THE ENGLISHWOMAN'S BEDROOM

THE ENGLISHWOMAN'S BEDROOM

Edited by Elizabeth Dickson
Photographs by Lucinda Lambton
Drawings by Paul Margiotta

SALEM HOUSE

SALEM, NEW HAMPSHIRE

First published
in the United States
by Salem House, 1985
A member of the Merrimack Publishers' Circle,
47 Pelham Road, Salem NH 03079

Library of Congress
Catalog Card Number
84– 52248

I S B N 0–88162–087–4

Printed in Great Britain

frontispiece
Lady Annabel Goldsmith's bedroom.
title page
A corner of the windowsill
in Lyn Le Grice's
Cornish country bedroom.

CONTENTS

Introduction

INTRODUCTION

I would like to thank all the many Englishwomen who allowed me into their bedrooms during the preparation of this volume, and especially those who kindly agreed to contribute. For the bedroom is invariably somewhere very personal; indeed it is often the most private domain within the home. By describing it in her own words, and by permitting photographs of it to be taken, each contributor has generously shared with the outside world not only her own particular taste in design but also a seldom-seen aspect of her personality. For the way in which the bedroom is perceived by the owner, the arrangement of the room itself and the bathroom or dressing rooms adjoining it, and what this represents to each woman, is a key to her character, private life and style.

As in a patchwork quilt, diverse interpretations of form, colour and design in this book compose the final structure of the chapters, from four-poster beds canopied in splendour to mattresses on the floor, from fantasies spun with spray-gun or tulle to a traditional setting, where, down the generations, the arrangement of the Englishwoman's bedroom is as welcome and comforting to its owner as pulling on an old cardigan.

Many and varied expeditions have been made in search of these bedrooms: nipping up turret stairs, clattering down into basements, swinging on hammocks, bouncing on mattresses hard or soft, plunging into rooms swamped in a deep litter of agreeable untidiness, tip-toeing into neatness, taking a candle to cottage attics, and catching a glimpse of the sea through Cornish bedroom windows.

The bedroom can be a haven for pillow talk, or for having breakfast on a tray with telephone and papers to hand, or it may be just somewhere to hang up your dressing gown before going to sleep; but what the bedroom most often offers to its owner, it seems, is her place of peace, somewhere she can always return to, comfortable, reassuring and individual.

While the bedroom has its roots in sleep it can take on many guises: a place of work, a bed-sitting room, part nursery, or a centre in which to hold court. The room can be a place for recuperation as well as rest and love, and its assembly can be the result of one person's whim or a compromise between partners.

The bed is the 'symbol of life', wrote de Maupassant, and all the Englishwomen in this book have given love and care to this particular symbol. The bedroom has also been described as the room in which we are born, cry, laugh and die. It is usually the last place we see at night and the surroundings we wake to next day, so it is a familiar place with something special for everyone. This is where we return to discharge our minds of care, recharge our energy, and, when we close our eyes, enter an even more private territory. In the bedroom we leave the world we know and, with or without four angels round our head, cross the frontiers into the world most private to us all, the land of dreams.   E.D.

GILL GOLDSMITH

Gill Goldsmith runs Loot, a shop in Pimlico which she inherited from a friend who was an antique dealer. She previously worked on a French fashion magazine, and was a freelance Paris correspondent for The New York Times. *She lives in a Victorian house in Chelsea, and her son and two daughters are now grown up.*

My obsession has always been to possess a room of my own. I had an agitated and nomadic childhood, and between the ages of ten and twenty I lost, in succession, all those things that children most treasure: my stamp collection, my birds' eggs, my pressed flowers, diaries, drawings and trinkets. They seemed to evaporate with every move and dwindled constantly, until at the age of twenty I possessed little more than a few items of clothing, a hideous crocodile handbag and a photograph of the school cat. I have been a magpie ever since.

Marriage should have provided me with the object of my desire, an 'English Lady's Bedroom', but since I shared it with a monstrously eccentric, chaotic, invasive gentleman – it was not. The cushions and bedcovers looked like dalmatians, covered in huge inkspots from leaky pens. The floor was constantly knee-deep in balls of screwed-up paper, rejects from his latest surge of inspiration. Huge wet footprints soaked the carpet, planted by a man too impatient to dry, who leapt from the bath taking half the water with him. The telephone was monopolised and the morning paper shredded like tickertape, with all the items of interest ripped out. Constant disagreement over the temperature of the room led to competitive opening and shutting of windows. The marriage hiccupped to a halt after fifteen years, and ended in an amiable divorce after which I finally achieved my lifelong ambition: a room of my own.

I acquired a large Victorian house in which I lived with my three teenage children, and shortly afterwards inherited a thriving antique shop called Loot, whose very name was a challenge to have a try at keeping the business going. This had a dynamic effect on my way of living, but at the heart of my activities was, at last, my own room. When I think of it the first image that comes to mind is a bolt-hole – not stark and private, but a haven of comfort and pleasure, pleasing to my eye, but a bit of a joke. As I was incapable of conceiving a pre-arranged decor, and too poor to afford a decorator, the bedroom, like the rest of the house, is an uncensored record of my acquisitions and aspirations.

Little of it has been affected by working in the antique business, although one or two irresistible or essential objects, like a huge lacquer mirror and a pair of bookcases, have sneaked in. I prefer large pieces of furniture to anything purpose-built, and in the same way I prefer pretty rugs on simple fitted matting – like that I can remove anything if I really have to. I can't describe my bedroom as decorated, just accumulated.

No master plan envisaged the flamboyant Victorian suite covered in gilded peacocks and lions' masks. It was just an unexpected present when I moved in, and sentiment will keep it there as long as I am, even though it is outrageously uncomfortable. It came from some minor guest room of the Nizam of Hyderabad.

The object which dominates the room is a picture over the fireplace. It represents a drowned girl lying on a beach, her flowing hair entwined with seaweed and shells. Gazing mournfully, a paw resting on her breast, is a charming dog of no identifiable breed. We pretend the girl is just asleep. I bought the painting at the insistence of the children from a removal firm in Brighton that we just happened to be passing. It was in the window advertising the merits of their long-term storage and in no way appeared to be for sale. Unable to resist the pleas of the children, I finally called the firm in question, and the charming old man who answered the telephone expressed amazement that anyone should covet her, and said she was indeed for sale, since no-one had claimed her for sixty years. She soon adorned the wall and subtly indicated the muted pink, ginger and sage green that are the basic colours of the room.

The origin of some of the smaller ornaments in the room is quite unusual. When I lived in France I had a good friend whose childhood had been much stranger than mine. At the beginning of the war there was a great exodus from Paris away from the Germans, and hundreds of children became separated from their parents and ran wild. She was one of these so-called vagabonds who lived on their wits, sleeping out and stealing their food. My friend was rediscovered by her mother at the end of the war, and subsequently became a well-known pop singer – but old habits die hard and she was an incurable scavenger. Any public property was in jeopardy if it caught her fancy. However, we discovered a more honest way of embellishing our homes. A wise old man called l'Abbé Pierre, a worker priest dedicated to the rehabilitation of Parisian tramps, had the excellent idea of offering a service of emptying people's attics for nothing. The daily crop of so-called rubbish was heaped up in an old

Gill Goldsmith

warehouse and sold by the tramps, who then kept the proceeds. The warehouse was on a pretty site on the banks of the Seine, and as the doors opened a horde of acquisitive housewives poured in and grabbed whatever caught their eye. The variety of wares was amazing, and the nearest tramp priced your booty on the spot. Naturally they had no time for our frivolous tastes. Gas stoves, chairs, pots and pans, anything utilitarian was exorbitantly priced, but ornaments, pictures, materials were scorned and sold for small change. To this day some of my most cherished possessions are things that came from there. A rare Delft tuliper, a cluster of silver birds – the native art from Dahomey, relic of some French colonial in Africa – a beautiful bronze Art Nouveau dish modelled as a girl's profile lying in a swirl of hair: all these remind me of my scavenging friend and the wily old tramps.

My bedroom has become a treasure chest, the resting place of all my

Extraordinary collection of objects form a compatible group around the fireplace. The oil painting over the mantelpiece is of a drowned seaweed-spattered girl and her dog; the two chairs are part of an extravagantly carved collection of furniture. The portrait behind the vase is of her son, Alexander.

dearest possessions. At the end of a day's work I rush upstairs, climb into bed and lie squarely within its four posts. The bed is a large squeaky edifice I found in the West Indies, where it came from a retired plantation owner who was only too happy to exchange it for a modern divan. Lace has replaced the clouds of mosquito nets that used to hang from its upper rails. The view from the window is, sadly, not the garden but a row of Victorian houses only mistily glimpsed through opaque lace curtains. The occasional furniture is mostly black lacquer, due to my fascination with Japanese art. The surfaces are so beautifully decorated with intricate patterns of birds and flowers that it is some compensation for their limited usefulness. They represent the core of a small collection of Japanese lacquer that I have gathered over the years.

Although this is my bedroom I don't necessarily consider it a retreat from company. I would have enjoyed the days when ladies had boudoirs, and entertaining while reclining was not considered risqué. Everything I enjoy most takes place in this room – I have my favourite books, my records, writing materials and an open fireplace banked by a couple of armchairs. I have to admit to an added luxury – a small adjoining room facing the garden where I actually sleep. Here there is no noise, no telephone, dark walls and Gothic furniture, with the added delight of waking up to the morning sun.

As I don't like clothes in the bedroom, apart from the piles that accumulate on the floor when I'm dressing in a hurry they live in a long corridor between the two rooms, and my bathroom next door is essentially just the bath and a long mirror for the last anxious look to see that everything is hanging together. Having few cosmetics I need no dressing-table, and usually stand by the window and make up in a small hand mirror.

Whenever I enter my bedroom I feel a sense of pleasure and security. The walls are the colour of wet plaster, a bleached rose, and the faded crewelwork curtains almost indistinguishable from the walls. With the lace curtains the impression is light but enclosed. Although I have few positive ideas about decoration I can detect my preferences by gazing about me. There are no bold colours, no geometric designs but a wealth of varied surfaces – there are beadwork curtains, embroidered screens, a patchwork quilt and woven carpets – everything seems to have some relief, and all the designs are flowery. The general impression seems to be of a suspended garden. I rarely have any fresh flowers unless some impulse sends me to pick a few in the garden, but bunches of dried or silk flowers are scattered all around, no doubt a sign of laziness.

Ultimately I think of my bedroom as home. My teenage children drove me out of the living room, and my own room has become the nerve centre of the house. I don't feel particularly territorial about it, and everyone gathers there. The moment I go away for a few days someone invades it. The children fight to sleep in it, and on occasions when I am at a safe distance my ex-husband relishes sneaking in too. This room is one of my chief delights, where I have spent some of the happiest moments of my life, and when I die, rather like the ancients, I would like to be buried with everything it contains.

LYN LE GRICE

Lyn Le Grice is the instigator of the current revival for stencilled interiors; she works principally with private clients, holds regular summer schools and offers a mail-order stencil service. She and her husband, Jeremy Le Grice, a painter, recently returned to Cornwall where they live and work in a watermill and its surrounding buildings.

I knew very well the basic feel of this bedroom, and that it should be clear and undemanding in terms of objects and decoration. The basic room is very much to my taste: a classic, straight-forward square shape, with one window that looks out across our small wooded valley and the stream leading round the corner to the sea two or three miles away.

Although I have found ways of coping with a great diversity of other people's exacting requirements for my stencilling work, paradoxically, when it comes to my own rooms, I find the whole idea much more complex. While I was doing it I would wake each morning with a different scheme for the bedroom in my head. You can become involved with your clients, seeing their needs as individuals very clearly, but when it comes to oneself it is hard to perform an equivalent task.

One draws strength from the familiarity of a room and this familiarity grows slowly, a process which is now beginning here. What one needs from a bedroom is a retreat, calm and peaceful; to achieve these qualities we have kept it looking like a white room, rather sparse, using cool linen for the materials of the canopy and curtains (and as a visual pun in juxtaposition with the oak linenfold screen behind the bed). The colour of the woodwork is a strange grey, much thinned with turps, which is compatible with the bronze and pink of the tufts of thrift that spread across the walls. This grey is used in the bathroom but there it has soft tones of blue and green pulled

across it, almost imperceptibly changing the mix, so the colours evolve into something more complicated.

Many of Jeremy's paintings are seascapes and, in a way, he used the bathroom walls like a canvas with the effect of the sea, not as powerful as a sea-painting but in the spirit of one. At first he put on a brilliant blue but this was too strong by night; the final result was arrived at after four or five further translucent coats, and the finished colour now works in all lights. This is an example of not treating colours with undue deference – what started with the most beautiful blue by daylight needed extra work to succeed in the artificial light of the night.

We have left the walls of the bedroom so that you can see traces of the layers of different colours left by the preceding generations of owners. Strong saxe blue and old rose revealed themselves when we started to prepare the walls, and these colours now show through in a transparent manner below a coat of thin old-fashioned white distemper. The finish is very slightly iridescent and most beautiful in early morning sunlight; it is made permanent by a coat of acrylic clear matt glaze.

Pale rooms like these do need a brave stroke of bolder tone; for instance, the black table which we brought in to add emphasis to the pale colours. Even the green binding of the bedspreads has a necessary bite of astringency. In our room in Gloucestershire, where we lived before, we found that a surprisingly strong viridian green arrested an atmosphere that might otherwise have become rather cloyingly sweet.

The rag rugs on the floor blend with the soft vole of the daubed grey paintwork. A weaver friend, Sue Marshall, worked very closely with me tying in all the colours from her sackful of linens (which were Sanderson seconds). The rags are bound at the ends and then cross-stitched at twelve-inch intervals across the surface.

When we moved into this house, we left it as far as possible as it stood for six months, wanting to get to know it and to understand its bone structure. It was Jeremy who took the decision about which of the many images I had for the stencilling was the right one, so I was let off the hook. From the many ideas I gave him, he latched on to my pattern of sea pinks, the thrift that grows on the cliffs around here, because their pale bleached colours are so Cornish and their shapes very relaxed. As always in my work, the surroundings and architecture are a prevailing influence on the subject matter and colouring, and here in the bedroom and bathroom the influence of the landscape, the rocks and seashore things like grey driftwood and shells is strongest. What we have finished up with is simple, strong and pretty, without, I trust, sentimentality.

The astonishingly powerful Cornish light has also been taken into account. The sea is all around us within a matter of a few miles, and the effect of the light is similar to that on a small island. If this had been the middle of the countryside the subdued colours might have looked rather dull. In England you can rarely use white successfully in the way you can on the Mediterranean, where you have all the contrasts of sun and shade. It's the same with blue, which you can use very well down here.

I love the shape of our bedroom, and the whole form of this house.

After living in a barn for twelve years, I found I developed a longing for the symmetry of a four-square layout of a house, with rooms laid out formally like a type of garden. In our barn in Gloucestershire, we had a bedroom in which a half-tester bed faced a huge window set into the sloping roof; we could lie in bed and look straight up into the towering beech trees which stretched along the line of the valley. Curtains did not seem necessary, for the leaves made a constantly moving pattern and acted as the most beautiful curtains one could imagine: what cloth could compete? In fact, here in Cornwall we have curtains, because the light is so strong and needs diffusing, and I find that looking at the play of light through the material gives me fresh pleasure each morning.

Both of us derive a frisson from disruption. Friends were astounded when we moved from Gloucestershire, so far from London, at the point when we appeared to be just settled. I have always been aware of the dangers of too much predictability, and I knew that once Wells Head had arrived at a point where it was landscaped, built and decorated, there was little remaining for us there except settling down to what Jeremy described as 'the endless process of manicure'. It was the constriction inherent in this view of the future, as well as signals of suburbia reaching even that lovely valley, that made us decide to up and off.

My mother has a nomadic streak even now; she always liked to be on the move, forever falling in love with impracticably large houses. At one point we had a vast place she had unearthed, surrounded by acres of fields although, curiously enough, in the middle of Surrey. We were offered the choice of several rooms, and at an early age I was able to take the initiative and do up my own room for the first time. It was at that house, I remember, that we found a beautiful Adam fireplace buried under piles of loose corn. Those times of moving house, and being given the encouragement to be individual, taught me the benefits to be gained from disruption: a kind of freedom in itself. Living here has really reduced my driven feeling, a part of myself that I am always in conflict with. I doubt whether we shall ever move again, because the pull westwards has been so strong and persistent for us both and there is not much further we can go in that direction, as we are now five miles from Land's End! It is also where all our six children most like to be.

Alsia, which we bought on impulse, is so refreshing. All its old, disused farm-buildings and the various terraced areas upon which the farm had been developed over the centuries, are on a gradual slope down from the edge of the fields to the old orchard, mill-stream and the mill, which was grinding flour for bread until the 1950s. You can always hear water running under the bridge and along the stream in front of the house. At the same time, business takes me away frequently. This provides the contrast which one needs for development.

This house is the calm centre at the axis of a very busy professional life. New schemes abound, and my work is always booked up well in advance with various different projects on the go. At this point Jeremy takes care of the management side of the business. It is a very fortunate partnership, as he is never too easy on me when he is looking over my designs and I rely

Lyn Le Grice

A *view through to the adjoining bathroom with stencilled floor, painted panels around the bath and a freestanding painted cupboard on the right.*

on him to pinpoint weaknesses. I seem to be obsessed with stencilling, which is why I do it. I find it so enlivening and, after all, this unending involvement with pattern is my livelihood, which I live happily with.

One thing about moving house is that you put everything, your ideas together with your possessions, back into storage, then gradually start testing them out again, retrieving what has weathered best. I do approve of this process of paring back, whether it refers to objects or processes in work, because there is a constant battle within me to keep everything in proper order, reflecting the stricter side of my nature. I am also drawn to beautiful, ornate things and wanting them around me. I hope that these two opposites, running together, produce something that is satisfactory — unique is too strong a claim.

I often work into the night when the telephone is silent and everyone has gone to bed. Jeremy tends to wake at six in the morning with his brain ticking fast, and by the time I have woken he has sifted everything through and has a list of questions ready for me. When I return from a job I am usually completely exhausted, emotionally and physically, and rather than unload all the paraphernalia, I just leave everything in the boot of the car until I want to get involved again. But, in a way, work is always germinating. The seeds of an idea are sown when you talk to a client, but the details and the drawings are attended to in the studio or office. I never draw in this bedroom, although we talk out some of the more complex questions here. Otherwise I try to keep my studio and office work away from the house altogether.

I have found I have great facility for making design and am sometimes shocked by the fact that it comes to me with such ease. I therefore take whatever time I can to draw from real things, in case this particular facility should take over too much. My obsession with pattern means that I compulsively want to rearrange everything I see in other people's rooms; I sit impatiently, and have to restrain myself from picking up an object and surreptitiously edging it a little closer to something near it, making a more effective grouping. I am constantly rearranging and refining things in our own house; it is a pleasure for me rather akin to gardening.

I am the most appalling perfectionist, but also too much of a realist to be in pursuit of perfection, whether in work or life generally; evolution and involvement are what count more. I horrified a client the other day when I said that I had only done two or three stencilling jobs that I really liked. I am seldom pleased with my work, but the drive, of course, is always to pull out the best I can.

Asked whether this is my ideal world I have to agree that it is not too bad; we have the pleasures of the country, the sea, and the buildings all taking shape, and now we have a civilised bedroom. When people come so near to Land's End they find themselves in a different world, remote and somehow un-English. It is a return to a point where we want to be.

Stencil motifs: the border round the window and a tuft of thrift, a seaside plant that grows on the Cornish cliffs.

PRINCESS NICHOLAS
VON PREUSSEN

Princess Nicholas von Preussen is the daughter of Lord and Lady Mancroft. Before her marriage to Prince Nicholas, a direct descendant of Queen Victoria, the princess worked as a kindergarten teacher, and later as a director of Piero de Monzi, a dress shop in Fulham. The von Preussens live with their two small daughters, Beatrice and Florence, in an eighteenth-century house in Somerset.

My bedroom is predominantly blue.

I have spent an important amount of time since I was about twelve in a house I love called The Cottage at Badminton, which is owned by the Duke and Duchess of Beaufort. A sitting room there is painted with *trompe l'oeil* panels and the curtains, sofa and chairs are in various different materials, all blue and white.

Since I first saw this room I have planned in my mind a similar room of my own. My husband, Nicholas, and I looked for our house in Somerset from the time that we got engaged in 1979, and when we found it two years later, we fell in love with it and bought it. The house is a bold and handsome Georgian one built mainly in 1756 in the local honey-coloured stone. I often travel abroad with my husband on business to Canada and America and to his vineyard in Germany, and this is a secure place to come back to.

As do most of the other rooms in the house, our bedroom has large Georgian windows – five of them; three in a bow facing west, and two facing south. The walls have *trompe l'oeil* panels. Our large four-poster bed on the east wall of the bedroom is deliberately high, so that on sunny

A cool reflection of the four-poster bed and out to midsummer greenery beyond. On the mantelpiece at the base of the mirror is a collection of blue and white porcelain, and beside it, on the right, a tapestry bell-pull.

mornings when we open the shutters we can look out of the windows over the garden down into the orchard and over the fields beyond. This is a spectacular view, heightened by the winding lane that threads through it: England at its best. At an early hour we discuss plans for the garden, the extension of the tree-planting programme, the rebuilding of the rose garden and the possibility of a tennis court next year. This is done while drinking strong Assam tea in bed and wrestling with the newspapers. Through the open windows comes the smell of the roses on the walls below, and the jasmine and honeysuckle which clings to the porch (or in my view supports it, as the porch is on the point of collapse) leading from the library into the garden. Through the frames of these same windows, when there is a storm, pours the rain.

The bedroom is bitterly cold in winter as the drawing room immediately below is as yet unused, and therefore unheated. Since moving here it has been a joke how much I have wanted bedroom curtains, and how completely secondary Nicholas thinks they are each time some new horror, such as dry rot or a leaking roof, presents itself. As the windows are shuttered, it is clear that the views expressed by me as to the necessity and importance of curtains are not entirely shared by my husband. But having already suffered two somewhat stark winters, and numerous discussions which have driven at least one of my three sisters quite mad, the curtains in blue ribbon English chintz will arrive in September. Next winter should see a rise in temperature in the master bedroom.

The white marble fireplace on the north wall of the bedroom came from the drawing room, for which we thought it too small. In winter Nicholas usually lights the fire before we bath in the evening, and we each check it until we go to bed. Finally, we put on a huge log which with luck will burn until dawn and help soften the blow of getting up the next morning.

Above the fireplace is a large Georgian mirror, which reflects the windows and an ever-increasing collection of blue and white china. At each end there is a large hourglass-shaped Delft pot with a lid, which Nicholas and I found together, and in between there are various Chinese porcelain teacups and saucers and a precious bit of Blind Earl given to me as a wedding present. The mirror also reflects our bed, which is hung with white spotted voile, designed and made locally by the Julian Workshop in Sherborne.

As the bed is so high, it is impossible for children and dogs to climb onto it. However, children and dogs require morning stories and biscuits, so I designed a hideous chipboard staircase which I covered in the same oatmeal cord as the carpet in the room. Up these three stairs each morning, with Nanny's assistance, climb our two daughters and two dachshunds, to indulge in their separate pleasures. The books are chosen from a special toy cupboard in a corner, which also contains baskets of old gaming chips and marbles. The dachshunds are unmoved by the stories. Sometimes the children eat the dog biscuits. They are kept on my bedside table in a tortoiseshell box with my initial on the lid, a present given to me one Easter by Nicholas. It is, incidentally, not Fabergé.

Princess Nicholas von Preussen in the newly-restored conservatory, which is shaped in a curve and leads from the dining-room of the house.

Our circular tables, one on either side of the bed, are both covered in nineteenth-century Welsh quilts. On my table, besides a lamp, the telephone and the biscuit box, I have an Edwardian mirror glass box which belonged to my mother's mother. In it I keep my manicure equipment along with some pink satin ribbon and a rather idiotic knitted silk hen, given to me, as I am reminded by the label attached to its leg, for Easter 1976. Next to the box sits a velvet mouse wearing a black tie which was presented to me at a May Ball. I am sentimental and keep things that some people (in particular my husband) would consider to be rubbish.

Although you can make at least two good piles of books on each of our tables there is, of course, never quite enough room. My piles include the telephone directory, the Country Garden Mail Order Catalogue, my address book, *Right Ho! Jeeves*, *The Best of Saki*, *Brewer's Phrase & Fable*, several biographies such as *Vita*, and, as there has always been, a Bible.

Nicholas's table is piled with magazines on motorbikes, boats, money and wine, as well as several other books on subjects not yet studied like lawns, herbs and fruit trees. He always has a P. G. Wodehouse or two which we sometimes read aloud to each other.

I keep few clothes in our bedroom as I have a little dressing room adjoining hung with photographs of both our families from childhood until now. However, to the left of the fireplace there is a large serpentine-fronted chest of drawers, bought in a sale about fourteen years ago. On top of this chest sit more photographs and a piece of Staffordshire china. Also a television set, which I dislike.

In the bow is a Regency sofa which belonged to my husband's great-grandmother, Adelaide the Countess of Iveagh. Into the cream ground floral crewelwork in which it is upholstered is woven her interlaced monogram.

At the moment, our pictures are mainly watercolours – some by my late uncle John Aldridge R.A., who was a professor at the Slade and whose watercolours and drawings I prefer to his oils – and also some aquatints, eighteenth-century engravings and flower prints. Above the chest of drawers there is a charming oil painting of my husband's great-great-grandfather, the German Crown Prince Frederick, at his marriage to Queen Victoria's eldest daughter Vicky, and on the opposite side of the fireplace, a watercolour of my dachshund Lily hangs next to a nineteenth-century bell-pull. Sadly no bell, and no-one to hear it either.

This bedroom is, however, dusted and cared for by Patrice and Chrystine, two local ladies who know where each photograph and piece of china should be, and exactly how I like the pillows on the bed, which were a wedding present from my brother Beano, to be placed.

The bedroom is at the west end of the house, and with my bathroom and dressing room leads from a small hallway in which my portrait by Howard Morgan hangs. These rooms are quite private, but if I have the door of my bedroom open I can hear just enough to know what everyone else is doing. If I stay in bed a little longer than usual, they come and see what *I* am doing.

Detail of crewelwork-covered sofa with monogrammed initials, and a blue silk Art Nouveau cushion embroidered with gold thread.

When I was twenty-one my parents gave me a trip around America as a birthday present. They also redecorated my bedroom as a surprise. It was. My mother unfortunately chose one of the few blue and white chintzes that I have ever disliked and so we were both angry and disappointed.

Since then, I determined to have what for me will be a blue and white bedroom of outstanding taste, charm and luxury. I am confident that in this large light room with its high ceiling and beautiful views this is what I will eventually achieve.

Beautiful balance of blue and white. Four-poster bed with a door on the left leading to the hallway, and to the dressing room on the right.

IRINA LASKI

Irina Laski shares her London flat with John Jesse, with whom she also runs an Art Nouveau antique business. After completing a degree in Philosophy and English nine years ago, she gradually started to deal in antiques, first in market stalls, and five years ago she opened the shop in Kensington with John Jesse.

Searching deep in cupboards and drawers for a pair of tights or a particular belt is the only hunting done in our jungle. It is essentially a peaceful jungle, and the mural which covers all four walls gives me a feeling of security and protection from the world outside, especially in the winter when the wind and rain can really batter at the windows. As well as being our private retreat which visitors rarely enter, this room is somewhere exciting, interesting and fun to be; a place where we can read, listen to music, watch television, chat or hold post mortems on the day's events. As Sunday afternoon is often our only time off during the week, we sometimes make the most of it by getting straight into bed after lunch with all the Sunday newspapers and spending the rest of the day there, reading and even having a light meal in bed.

I have always felt that a bedroom is an ideal room for visual experimentation. My previous bedrooms have all been very white and stark and I wanted a change. The idea of a jungle was a sudden and very strong urge to go in a completely opposite direction. I am sure that the room's size, height and view had something to do with it. It is a very large and light room with wonderful views over the rooftops of London, and I felt its marvellous scope and potential overcame the risk of it becoming claustrophobic and depressing. Luckily John's sister, Joanna Campion, is a professional painter and muralist, and once the idea of a warm and

The silken, padded kimonos embroidered with stylised flowers, waves and carp from the owners' collection disguise a fretwork screen in the foreground and are strewn on the divan bed. Animals at home in their top-floor jungle lair include iguanas on the bamboo dressing-table, a ceramic monkey on the corner table, a leopard prowling across a chenille cushion cover, and a tiger woven into the rug.

exotic jungle was conceived, she instinctively understood and interpreted the idea in her own style very successfully. We chose only four colours, and decided that the ceiling had to be a rich tropical ultramarine sky of great intensity: an antidote to the concrete jungle outside.

Another jungle activity that takes place in my bedroom is that of dressing. John is often amused to find me trying out various ensembles, experimenting with a new look or outfit. A while ago we discovered that I had so many clothes that we decided to build a fitted wardrobe over the entire end wall, which Joanna then painted over in her inimitable style. We deliberately tried to disguise the joins and door cracks so as not to interfere with the look of the room as a whole. There is a special tall section in the wardrobe which houses our kimono collection. John and I find that kimonos are not only beautiful works of art to look at, but also wonderful to feel and wear. We both have everyday ones that we wear all the time and our favourite ones for when the mood arises. Unfortunately it is impossible to contain everything in this built-in wardrobe, especially as I am constantly adding to it, so we have three other free-standing cupboards in the room. Our travels abroad would be sadly lacking without the excitement of the hunt for exotic 'trophies' to bring back. The twenty-foot Indian turbans and saris in the most vivid blues, reds and oranges create not only an incredible richness of colour, but conjure up a wealth of memories and adventures.

It also seems a shame to hide away inside a cupboard the wonderful array of colours and shapes of the handbags and sunglasses that I collect, so I try to leave the cupboard doors open and hang the bags on any knobs or handles that I can find. As well as being useful accessories they make great decorative objects to look at, and I am constantly amazed at the inventiveness and imagination of the different designs.

This brings me to my favourite visual spot—the bamboo dressing-table. Although I am not altogether keen on too much bamboo furniture, a few select pieces seemed an obvious choice and looked in their element in the jungle, their natural habitat. I enjoy draping and covering the dressing-table with lots of my favourite pieces to give a wonderful overgrown appearance. The light from the hanging lamp, with its enamelled parrot, gives a perfect glow to all the beads in the jewel casket. I've always loved the idea of a casket filled with secret treasures that you would find hidden away in a fairy princess's castle. My wish came true when John found the perfect Arts and Crafts piece, ideal for cramming so full of glittering costume jewellery that it cascades over the sides.

As John and I are dealers in Art Nouveau and Art Deco, the decoration of where we live seems to evolve naturally around the objects we find. As every day is spent looking for things to buy and sell in our shop, it is inevitable that I come across really beautiful pieces, and the problem is which I can keep and which I should sell. There is a constant flow of objects in the flat, because we sometimes enjoy certain things at home for a while before selling them, but the furniture remains static as it would be too much of an upheaval to keep changing it around. Besides which I rarely see furniture that I would actually like to live with, as it has to

A blue parrot in the Handel hanging glass lamp looks down on an Aladdin's Cave mixture of jewellery and ornaments on the dressing-table. Necklaces garland the mirror, and an Arts and Crafts casket spills over with brooches, bracelets and hair-combs.

Dressed for the jungle, Irina Laski in a richly textured kimono, against an equally fantastic background of painted leaves.

combine a certain stylishness with comfort and practicality, so anything delicate like French Art Deco lacquer is avoided. Although I appreciate rooms that adhere strictly to one style or period, my own taste is far too eclectic, and I prefer to surround myself with pieces that I love rather than confining myself to what should fit. I'm definitely more of a mixer than a matchmaker, and I love to discover odd combinations that work.

A jungle in the living room too might have become rather restrictive and overpowering, and I really enjoy the contrast between our simple Art Deco sitting room with its magnolia walls and cream leather furniture and our much warmer and cosier bedroom. When moving from one room to the other I love the feeling of going somewhere completely different. As I climb the stairs to the bedroom I feel as if I were leaving the cares and efforts of everyday living far below and entering a different world. There is no glare and no harsh lights, just enough of a glow from our Art Glass lamps to read by. This room is a wonderful retreat – a place to relax and unwind – and I immediately throw off tight constricting clothes and climb into loose comfortable silk pyjamas and a beautiful soothing kimono.

This collection of handbags and sunspecs ranges from Art Deco to Op Art.

VISCOUNTESS ASTOR

Lady Astor, in front of an oil painting by an unknown artist in about 1884: 'The Astor Family in a New York Interior'.

Lady Astor is the wife of the fourth Viscount Astor, a businessman, and they live in a red-brick Jacobean manor house in Berkshire. She is the founder and sole designer of a jewellery business in Knightsbridge, and she has worked since the age of seventeen when she opened the shop under the professional name of Annabel Jones. Lady Astor has five children under the age of fourteen, all of whom live at home in the country with her.

I love ostentation. The gaudier the better. I wear masses of jewellery, except when I am in jeans with my family, and I love diamonds; the bigger the rocks, the more they please me. I like my bedroom to have a certain opulence, a combination of larger-than-life furniture, richness of colour and warmth. The contradiction in all this is that I have always tried to be a non-conformist, yet in the end I return to the traditional. I read a lot of Russian literature when I was fourteen, and the Russian stories, particularly those of Turgenev, rooted in me from early on a heady feeling for the flamboyance and romance of life. And a degree of recklessness. For I am a gambler, and an opportunist.

My life is spent looking forward, and I recall little about the countless rooms I have lived in. I ignore the past, although mine has always been happy, because my mind is filled with what happens now and projects for the future. I see life as fun and one enormous giggle.

My husband succeeded to his title when he was sixteen, at which point he moved to this house with many of the things from Cliveden, the family seat, which is now owned by the National Trust. I would agree that the name Astor is synonymous with wealth, style and glamour from an outsider's point of view, but in the nine years since I came to live here I have adjusted to treating all these beautiful objects of museum quality as I would any familiar furniture. I feel very strongly that we are custodians of the family heritage, but we use things for the purpose they were intended for, and try not to worry about damage. My children do not break things clumsily, and they have a respect for our things that is innate in their upbringing. I do not believe you should put possessions on a pedestal.

Comfort is the most important element of a house. The bedroom must be warm and inviting, and the sitting room must have the most comfortable chairs. I love spaces with secluded corners where people can sit and talk in one part, with other people playing cards in another part, and the feeling that you are able to lounge around, feet up on everything. I am all in favour of that.

In my mind's eye I imagine a bedroom that is perfect down to the very last drip of paint, even though I am naturally untidy, but of course the room is a compromise. The difficulty is deciding how to make a room that is not boring yet copes with all the ugliness of clothes lying about, a place for make-up, heated rollers and so on.

In spite of my love of colour, I initially launched off into another idea and this room began as an all-white bedroom, a sea of white with plush white damask. All most adventurous, I thought at the time, but it became rather a Mrs Haversham setting, bleak and slightly strange except in the sunny midsummer months. After five years the room started to undergo a slow change, and the white Polish bed was changed to its present arrangement. The posts, which I had made by our carpenter, were covered in silk, and I used a hanging flower-basket of wire attached upside down to the ceiling and covered with chintz to make the effect of the crown.

Strictly my own invention are the bed hangings, which took me over nine months to make. They were put together from several sources: the thistle pattern chintz from one London decorator and the fringe from another, and the pink poplin trimming from the local country draper. The curtains were made from Peter Jones' damask and were white to begin with, but thankfully have yellowed with age and mellowed with dust. I abhor net curtains, and instead there are Venetian blinds made of mahogany which I defiantly painted white, although most people miss the point and think they are plastic.

The bedcovers were originally the heavily embroidered silk sheets used by the Astor family long ago, as was our bearskin travelling rug which has a pocket to put your feet into. The tapestry cushions on the bed and the picture of St James's Palace over it are all from Cliveden, and the tiger skins draped over the valance were shot by my grandfather, Sir Bede Clifford, in India sometime between the Wars.

Somewhere back in my childhood I may have come across a Polish bed, and possibly it had something to do with my mother's family who were all very romantically inclined. From the age of six I would accompany my mother on some of her travels, because it was then that she began to do up houses professionally, and this was my introduction to the possibilities of beautiful things. She is incredibly imaginative and was an early lesson in

style. I would not use the word 'taste' in reference to her, as to me this has a sheep-like quality.

My grandmothers were also an early influence, and although I have a bad memory I could never forget their houses. Enid Bagnold, my father's mother, lived in a huge house at Rottingdean in Sussex, a magical place built in the Lutyens style. It was a maze of clutter and objects, some of which, like her Georgian black lacquer, reflected her love of the nearby Brighton Pavilion. She was totally unconventional. There were always masses of theatrical people passing through, and there seemed to be hundreds of bedrooms, but for some reason I was put to sleep on a bed in the bathroom with a floor of shiny green linoleum. My other grandmother, Lady Clifford, had a craze for gilt, and with her rich, heavy cream and white damask curtains that were so much of the Thirties, there was always a tendency for things to be overdone or wildly exaggerated. These were the ingredients for the development of my own style. A further ingredient was the frugality and discipline I learnt in childhood, which, on looking back, have been a great help in making a success of my life.

One of my early ventures into decorating was when I first had my own home. The bedroom was based around a Chinese wallpaper given to me by my mother, which was a pale grey painted with flowers and butterflies. I made my bedcover and the trimmings, all in dark yellows, and the local carpenter built a bed in the shape of a four-poster with a canopied top hung from the ceiling.

If I am doing up a room other than the bedroom green always seems to come into play, although it is not a colour that I really like. Yet it is a colour that assails the senses, or so it seems, because in this beautiful house surrounded by gardens and trees we have four rooms in varying shades of green. For example, my bathroom is now painted an apple-green rock marble, and my husband's dressing room is in deeper shades of green painted to a fake tortoise-shell finish.

I have a horror of pale blues and pinks in bedrooms, even though the curtains of my bed are picked out with bits of pink. The concept of an insipid, sugary Englishwoman's bedroom, all predictably frilly, is something that I cannot bear. I do not like all those materials by the lady who does the little prints. The style of my bedroom is more sensual than I believe you find with the typical English four-poster, but the bed hangings give me the same pleasure of being able to look up from the pillows to an enclosure of materials overhead.

Many present-day Englishwomen's bedrooms appear to be an exclusively female preserve, while the male dressing room is a place of deep comfort and dark cosiness, but a sadly separate territory. I have consciously created a setting for my husband in our bedroom. He has very definite views to which I always adapt, since I could not live with someone who felt they had no part in the character of the house. He has less concern for the bedroom than I do, because for him it is simply a place to sleep, though he does like to have a chair for his clothes, the dog's basket and a feeling of space, as well as basics like the telephone within reach of the bed and a good reading lamp. I believe all those things matter much

On the table between the windows stands a plaster bust of Enid Bagnold by Henri Gaudier-Brzeska. The oil painting, by John Van Der Lyn, is of John Jacob Astor's family; the Bessarabian rug on the floor was a present from Enid Bagnold, Lady Astor's grandmother.

Looking through to the bedroom, the walls are decorated with china from a Worcester dessert service with painted landscapes. On the ebonised and black lacquer cabinets, a pair of Chamberlain's Worcester vases with covers.

more to a man than the colour of the curtains; men do not occupy bedrooms in the way that most women do. I retreat to mine for complete relaxation and to empty my mind of thoughts, and when I am not working I make the time to lie flat on my bed in the afternoon to rest and read. Though my bedroom is respected as an area of privacy in a house filled with such a large family, it is a centre of activity at seven-fifteen in the morning when we gather for tea on the bed with the children and dogs all bounding in on us.

Years ago when I was trying to do my A levels in Cambridge, I gave huge lunch parties in my bed-sitter almost every day of the week, although we ate only cheese and biscuits; it was the same need for conversation and laughter and a lot of people around me. I have always been gregarious. Strength of character made me want to do something with my life, as well as a lack of self-confidence and a need to be noticed. I grew up the centre

of attention and with great love in my family, and I wanted to continue being noticed for myself.

When I was sixteen I had to apply my mind to making money in an interesting job, and as I had done a correspondence course in precious and semi-precious stones when I was fifteen, I decided to design and retail jewellery. I approached a friend of my father's called Colin Crewe, who backed my venture, with the result that Jones opened when I was seventeen. The first three years were very tight, working long hours with little reward. Today I have about half a dozen people working in the shop at Beauchamp Place and another fifteen in the workshops, but I remain the sole designer. All my work is done either at my desk in the sitting-room at home, or in the basement office in London. I always travel to London by train, getting to my desk at eight-thirty in the morning and leaving at six-thirty. These spates of work run for two or three days a week, with spells of three weeks or so off for recuperation after I have finished a project, because I can only work to deadlines and would never do an endless nine-to-five routine.

I design two collections of jewellery a year, and every season I travel abroad to look at all the designers' collections to get an idea of the new fashions, because my stock has to be contemporary but at the same time not too way out. I now have an antique jewellery side to the business as well. Our customers are the very rich. People from different parts of the world have varying enthusiasms, but the English particularly love sapphires, perhaps because they are blue.

I am so absorbed in the interest of my work, which also produces high earnings, that I think I have greater enjoyment out of life and more freedom than some of my girlfriends. The money means that I can organise my home and my work life as I want, and delegate the mundane routine to others. I forget about work when I get home, and this is greatly due to my husband's help. He realised early on that if I was going to run a home and a business, these things had to be kept separate or I would succeed at neither. He takes great interest and enormous pride in what I do, and I could not manage as well without him to steer me in the right direction. I would never get a good night's sleep if I were to worry about what was going to happen the next day.

I have doggedly worked away and always ended up with what I wanted. I believe that if you expect a lot from life somehow the opportunities present themselves and then must be grasped without delay whatever the consequences.

Yet my first thoughts and loyalties are to family life, and I adore being surrounded by masses of children of all ages. I do not banish nursery life behind a green baize door. Recently we had thirteen children staying in the house, and about the same number of adults. One night, after a long, marvellous evening, I unsuspectingly came up to my bedroom at two in the morning to find that the children had made us the most enormous apple-pie bed. It not only had clothes in it, but fruit and vegetables and every other sort of gunge stuffed down the sheets, and soda water sprayed everywhere. We slept under blankets on the bare mattress. It was an uncomfortable night, but all part of life in our bedroom.

Needlepoint and tapestry cushions, originally from the Astor family home at Cliveden.

JEAN SHRIMPTON

Jean Shrimpton is an hotelier. She left school at sixteen and during the 1960s became the legendary photographic model with a face and style synonymous with that decade. Later, she retired from the modelling business to become an antique dealer and manage a smallholding. Now, with her husband Michael Cox, she runs the Abbey Hotel at Penzance in Cornwall. They have a five-year-old son, Thaddeus.

To me the bedroom represents a sanctuary, as running an hotel is an all-consuming job and it is very important that I have somewhere to relax and get things back into perspective. Not surprisingly, one of the most important assets is a really good bed. I bought mine a long time ago at Heal's, at what seemed at the time an enormous price, but I have never regretted it.

One of the other things that brings me really great pleasure is beautiful linen, which can also be expensive, but I buy it in the local salerooms and I think I have enough to last me the rest of my life. I also try to use embroidered sheets in the hotel, in spite of the laundry problems. I am continually impressed by the beauty of hand-made things and the obvious care that went into them, and am also surprised that, given the advance of modern technology, the quality of goods produced today is often so poor and dull in design.

When I first came to the Abbey for lunch many years ago, I was struck by the peaceful, timeless quality I found here. It was like opening a door into an era in which I felt completely at home. The building itself, which dates from the fifteenth century and overlooks Penzance harbour, is quite beautiful, and most of the rooms have very pleasing proportions. At the time I first came here, both the furniture and the guests were fine old

Jean Shrimpton with a favourite wooden Buddha on the table beside her.

antiques, but rather on their last legs. I had the fantasy that when I grew old it would be the perfect place for me.

When we heard that the hotel was to be sold we were very reluctant to see it change, and for better or worse we bought it. Unfortunately, fantasy and reality are often light years apart, and the reality in our case was that people did actually expect good beds, central heating and so on, which we then had to set about providing. In doing so, we hope we have enhanced the place and not lost the elusive quality that first attracted us to the Abbey; certainly it is much more comfortable now.

In decorating the rooms in the hotel we were often constrained by economic necessity, which in retrospect I believe to be of fundamental importance in achieving an individual style. If you can simply afford to walk into expensive shops and buy a complete co-ordinated look, it tends to reflect your cheque book rather than your style. Style is not a question of money, it is more a reflection of your personality.

The Abbey is not an hotel in the conventional sense, any more than I am a conventional hotel owner. The atmosphere is very relaxed and the place often seems rather empty; there is very little obvious service, although there is always someone in the building if you want something, but you may have to seek them out. This lack of pressure and the feeling of being in someone's house can be a little disconcerting for people at first, but they usually come to enjoy it.

The flat in which we live adjoins the hotel. It is very small and extremely cluttered with papers and toys belonging to my son Thaddeus, who is five. This often drives me crazy, so I make a concerted effort to keep the bedroom in a tranquil and relatively tidy state.

It is a typical Cornish cottage bedroom, with one window that looks out down the steep hill to Penzance harbour and across the bay to St Michael's Mount. The thickness of the old wall makes a deep window seat. The room is painted a strong blue, simply because I like the colour. It has a low, sloping ceiling, and the beams at either end are painted white. Contrary to what one would expect, it is not in the least bit cold, but blue can look chilly if used with white so I have used splashes of red to warm it up. It is rather an odd choice, but it is a colour that I like very much and that I cannot wear, except in shoes. It always makes me happy to see red feet, and similarly I keep finding ways to incorporate splashes of red into the bedroom. I am constantly searching for paintings with red in them, but this seems to be easier to find in modern paintings, to which I am not so drawn – although a Matisse would be an exception, of course.

I also like round tables covered with quilts or fabric. Mine is covered with an embroidered silk Chinese shawl in pinks and cream. On it stand some of my favourite objects: a fat ivory hippopotamus which is lovely to hold, and an ivory figure of Kuan Yin, who seems to preside peacefully over the whole table. I do not have many photographs around, just a couple of Thaddeus. One of the most special objects in the room is a silver and enamel Art Nouveau frame which holds a photo of him when he was younger; others include a shagreen case containing a set of drawing instruments and a charming little pierrot figure into which I put flowers.

I always take care to have lots of flowers in the room and am particularly fond of old-fashioned roses, ranunculus and lilies of the valley. We have a collection of about forty old-fashioned roses which grow against the wall in the herb garden opposite the hotel. One of my great pleasures is to see the hotel full of flowers; conversely, one of the great irritations is the chore of changing them every two days, which means petals all over the hotel and lots of stagnant water.

I really would have liked my bedroom to have a beautifully polished, mellow wooden floor with rugs on it, but unfortunately I am landed with chipboard. I do like wood that glows and has the patina of much-handled leather. One of my favourite pieces of furniture is the cupboard next to the bed. I bought it from Geoffrey Bennison, whom I knew when I lived in his hotel in Earl's Court in the early 1960s.

Kuan Yin figure carved in ivory presides over a group of nautilus shells and an ivory hippo. A church candle stands on the left.

The carved oak bedhead in our room is another example of economic necessity being used as a positive force. It in fact started life as a fireplace surround which my husband took apart and rebuilt to a different shape. He then added a padded headboard insert, which I covered in red Indian fabric. The material cost me four pounds in the saleroom. The fireplace cost fifty pounds, but I think the finished effect looks as if it is worth considerably more.

Obviously we all have a concept of a truly ideal bedroom. For me this would definitely incorporate a log fire, in spite of the work it involves, because I love the lingering smell of woodsmoke and the life a fire brings to the room. It also provides a focal point around which to work. My ideal room would probably also include crewelwork curtains and two very comfortable faded armchairs, a beautiful view of the countryside with cornfields in summer, and the smell of honeysuckle.

View from the window; the hotel is built on a steep hill and over-looks Penzance harbour.

VIRGINIA WETHERELL

Virginia Wetherell is an antique dealer and actress who is married to the actor Ralph Bates. They live with their two young children, Daisy and William, in a Victorian Gothic house in west London.

Ralph and I are both actors. We both like playing, and this is our set. I become what I see around me, and as the bedroom is about playing the ribbons and posies on the four-poster are simply part of the game. Yet, at the same time, the style comes naturally to me.

There has been no matching of skirting-board to ceiling colour, and fiddling about with little swatches of fabric toning this with that, although this is how I set about things for clients whose homes I help with. Here it is different, because the room is me and the atmosphere is sensual and warm. This is style – nothing else – and it has to do with artifice. A little artifice is a good thing.

Although our world is like a stage, of course there is also the reality. I feel that the bedroom serves three basic purposes: to sleep in, to make love in, and to be ill in. These are the three major things, because the daily routine is relentless – I am either working or looking after the children, and we are more often out of the room than in it.

This room rekindles romance, and as Ralph is away a lot it is all the more important that he returns to a place which remains a dark, peaceful nest. He is a restless sleeper and I hate the morning light, so we have thick velvet curtains and the comforting atmosphere is quite the opposite of the hotel rooms where he stays when he is working. There was a weekend, last summer, when I joined him in Sweden where he was making a film, and we spent the whole weekend trying to block out the light in the hotel windows with newspaper.

*An antique brass bed dressed
with pink silk ribbons and posies
turns into a four-poster.*

Once we had a sugar-pink bedroom, but it felt as if we were folded into a blancmange. Faded pink has always been my favourite colour – I'll rough up new pink espadrilles at the beginning of summer purposefully to make them appear faded and inconspicuous – but pink is too obvious for a bedroom. The tones in here are closer to shadowy peach.

Everything in the bedrom was accumulated gradually, with the furniture easing into the most comfortable places. The objects were found in markets or junk shops during the last thirty years, or were presents from friends. Some are rather a joke, like the Andy Capp slipper used as a door stop, or the fluffy pink mules I was given, but the setting is intentionally over the top. It is a bit brothelly and baroque – sensual but not sleazy. Objects like the bead curtains and a mirror by the bed are right for playing a courtesan character, and the most romantic lighting of all for making love is candlelight. We put candles on the floor on either side of the bed. I notice that other people also have the same Klimt print of lovers in their bedrooms, and the picture is undoubtedly very erotic and gentle. However, the architecture of life changes so much when you have children. Those late mornings when I used to nip down to put the kettle on, then back into bed with a cup of coffee, just fade into the past.

My style has been constant. As a child I used to gather shells and dry flowers, and in my house now there are influences from the years when my family lived in Mauritius: a faintly Somerset Maugham atmosphere of fans, verandahs, sea-bleached colour, a stillness in the heat. Later, when I was at drama school in London, I would go to Church Street market on Saturdays and buy things for a penny, then two-and-six, then five shillings. Later on, when I started work, it was a desk for five pounds.

My flat was just the same then as now – lots of lace. Sometimes when people came to the place they would laugh, but put it this way – the people I like, like this style, and girlfriends are usually bowled over; it seems that women often hanker after the same kind of splendour.

This bedroom creates confidence, although when you have been married for as long as we have, then, quite honestly, you are not putting on a show every night. Even so, it has always been very important to me to create and maintain an impression.

There was a time when I spent many days lying in bed here after a major operation. On my return from hospital, where everything was so colourless, I walked into this room and burst into tears. It was so pretty; it looked to me like fairyland. Then, in all the hours that followed, I had time to look at the different objects in the room, and remember where they came from and the people behind them. When the children are ill they are allowed into our bed, and they love it; sharing the soft pillows and the Edwardian wicker tray with its fold-down legs is for them the most tremendous treat.

I made the bed hangings and put the lace in the room on a sudden impulse. Ralph had been away for a long stretch, and he was due back in two days' time. We had been in the house for at least four months, but the original red and gold flock wallpaper was still there. So, I decided that I would make the room very sexy for Ralph's return, and that sticking lace around the walls would help to capture this mood. I happened to have some terracotta-coloured wallpaper which I had bought for the children's room, so up it went onto the walls, and the ceiling was given a coat of magnolia. The paper is one of the early Laura Ashley prints, a cliché now, but it has faded pleasantly and forms a good background. Then I just played with the lace, hanging it everywhere – you can see the patterns much better when they are backed with colour rather than spread on white.

Occasionally things in the room may be replaced, because if someone comes into my shop and asks for a particular bead purse, say, and the telephone bill has to be paid, then the purse disappears from my dressing room and something else is brought home instead. A picture from the Flea Market may have a particular appeal for me, so it rests for a while here on its journey to the shop.

The bed came from the dentist next door to me when I lived in Holland Park, years ago. Sitting in his chair one day I gave a yelp, not from the drill but from the glimpse of a piece of brass emerging through the bushes in his garden. When I asked him what it was, he replied that it was some awful old bed; we did a swop, bartering twelve towels for the bed all thickly encrusted with mud and leaves.

A brass bed is wonderfully romantic and timeless, and it lends itself to dressing up as a four-poster in the way I have done. But none of the repro ones look right to me. Brass beds have to be old, with the brass none too highly polished. The aim is for a slightly tatty, decadent air, worn but clean. This has a new divan on it and a mattress, and five foot six is a snug width but with plenty of room to house all the family. I don't know why, but I just couldn't be satisfied with a straightforward Heal's bed.

Our ultimate luxury would be to have clean sheets top and bottom, every single day, but it is not practicable at the moment. The upkeep of all this old linen and lace takes time, but I quite enjoy the ironing.

Apart from the bed, which is the top priority in a bedroom, the right lighting is vital. We got rid of the centre light here, and hung three antique lamps over the little round table. The shades are favourite ones, and in order to see them all at once I hung them at different levels, although if I had my way there would be at least ten more, to make a waterfall of light. Although we like low romantic lighting, we do also like to read and know roughly what colour we are getting dressed in, so Ralph has put the system onto dimmers.

A so-called professional decorator would have a heart attack seeing this place. The lights, for instance, are in all the wrong places as far as convention goes, but it is agreeable to us. I need only a dim light on the dressing-table because when I make up before going out somewhere special, the effect I'm after for myself is soft and flattering, which will give me confidence as I sit somewhere dark at dinner. I want to see myself as I'd

Virginia Wetherell

like others to see me, and I'm not interested in standing in the kitchen under a fluorescent light with smudged mascara.

It is important and comforting to us to have a multitude of photographs of the family in the room, and there is a crowd of them near the bed, mostly in old frames. There is a stunning black lacquer frame painted with daisies, but the most treasured is the one in the shape of a gilt butterfly whose wings are on either side of the photograph.

Butterflies have always held a fascination for me, and my experiment of sticking a child's blue butterfly transfers onto a glass lampshade worked to great effect.

Almost the most precious object in the room is the painting in the corner of the girl with the rose garlands, the provenance of which is unknown. I do not know why this picture provokes such an obsession in me. The silk flowers crowning the mirror are also part of the game, because in my fantasy these roses are the same ones as the girl in the picture is carrying, just as the spotted muslin dress on the door is the same kind of garment as that worn by the lady in the painting further along the wall. She is stooping to pick up a shell by the seashore. Surely this lady is how we would all like to be? She is, in my imagination, free and confident. She is surrounded by nice smells, which we long for living in a city, and I can feel the temperature of the ocean and the soft breeze around her. The marble figure, which I sold to Biba and bought back again after their demise, the girl who is part of the china dish and the figures in the little painting on glass, all seem to be images of the same free female spirit who

A Belle Epoque statue which saw much life at the Biba store during the 1970s, a French glass lamp, an English bamboo writing desk and a tin toy butterfly on wheels are gathered under the owner's favourite picture in an oak and copper Art Nouveau frame.

emerged about eighty years ago. Each is based on the same idea of woman, and it is her with whom I privately identify.

Despite my passion for coloured glass and the different kinds of lace, whether it is the ultimate pillow in Victorian broderie anglaise with the pattern worked into a star, or our three different bedcovers – the shawl one, the lace and the one stitched with roses – I must add that there are times when Ralph draws the line and threatens to leave home. This is when he finds me carting yet another box of frills up the stairs to our room and, much as he enjoys the voluptuous setting, he says with trepidation, 'What happens if you die first, and I am left with all this to look after?'

One of several round tables in the bedroom, this one is dressed with three lace cloths. More antique ribbon lace screens the windows. The three opaque glass shades are Victorian, fitted with pale pink bulbs and glittering glass bead fringes. Other objects in the still life composition are a mirror with hand-painted flower frame, bead purses, an Edwardian rosebud china menu holder, an Austrian Art Nouveau dish and an Italian wedding breakfast token of sugared almonds wrapped in pink-spotted net.

LADY ANNABEL GOLDSMITH

Lady Annabel Goldsmith is the second daughter of the eighth Marquess of Londonderry. She lives with her second husband, the financier Sir James Goldsmith, and their three children Jemima, Zacharias and Ben-Ben in a Queen Anne house on the edge of Richmond Park in Surrey.

I believe it is a fact that most people choose one room in the house as the place where they spend most of their time and feel most comfortable, even though it might not be the most decorative one. I suppose it is rather like domestic pets who will invariably pick one place in the house in which to sleep, hide their bones, have their kittens and so on.

In my case, this particular room happens to be my bedroom, although I am sure that for many people a more likely place would be a den, a little library or sitting-room or somewhere open-plan. As the bedroom is usually a very private room, it is the one room one often has to ask to see, and nobody else ever takes me into their bedroom in quite the same immediate way they are invited here. Mine is almost the main room of Ormeley Lodge, and is such a perpetual meeting-place of family and friends and all the animals that I cannot think why it is not more grubby than it already is.

I cannot really remember when my bedroom became the most important room to me, but I rather think it started when I was married to Mark Birley and we lived in an enchanting house called Pelham Cottage in South Kensington. Unlike my present bedroom at Ormeley Lodge, that one was not particularly beautiful, despite Mark's exquisite taste. I suppose the best feature of that room was the huge bed which became the centre of the household, with my three other children by Mark doing their homework on it, the dogs and cats a permanent spread-eagled feature, and where later in the evening everyone climbed into bed to watch television. We even had dinner in bed.

We lived there for twenty-two years, until various changes forced me to move. Mark and I had separated, and I had produced two new children by Jimmy Goldsmith. We had outgrown Pelham Cottage and I had fallen in love with Ormeley Lodge, with its beautiful rooms and wonderful rural atmosphere. I quickly discovered that our new bedroom was one of the most beautiful rooms in the house.

The space ran the width of the house with long Queen Anne windows on either side of it. The fireplace had been blocked in and the room seemed a bit sad and unlived-in. How was I to warm it up? I remember thinking that it all seemed very large, rather like the bedrooms of my childhood at Mount Stewart, the Londonderry family home in Ireland, and at Wynard, which is now the family seat in the north of England; I wondered whether I would be able to adapt to a large bedroom after a small cosy one.

Also, and by far the most alarming, was a letter that arrived, written by a well-meaning old man who had spent his childhood at Ormeley. Sadly, I cannot print the letter as it is too long, but the gist of it was to tell me how happy he had been there when his father was the family groom, and how happy he hoped we would be. Was I aware, he continued, that a terrible crime had been committed at Ormeley in the early eighteenth century? An Italian count had been brutally murdered, and the staff in the old man's day used to hear the 'bump, bump, bump' of the body being dragged down the stairs. He did not know where the body was buried, but he believed that the room in which the crime had been committed (he proceeded to explain which window it was) had been my new bedroom.

I felt rather queasy about the information, but everyone else to whom I read the letter, at different times, simply roared with laughter. A few months later, fortunately, a former tenant of the house who knew much about its past history was able to put my mind at rest by telling me that the room directly above mine was the one in which the death had occurred.

One of the many interesting historical facts about Ormeley is that Mrs Fitzherbert also lived here for a while, and it was she who built on this part of the house, with my bedroom in it. After her morganatic marriage to the Prince of Wales in 1785, they spent their honeymoon here, and during the winter months they became snowed in. It is a romantic assumption, but all the same it does seem very likely that this house had been their secret love-nest for some years before their wedding.

With the help of my decorator Tom Parr, we started to plan the bedroom, because I soon realised that a great deal of careful thought had to be put into making a large room both cosy and lived-in. I chose what I thought, and still do think, is one of the prettiest chintzes that exist, a combination of pansies and roses with small flowers, which vaguely reminded me of a guest bedroom in my grandmother's house. (The first material I was shown had a rather icy, pale green pattern, but this made me think of glacier mints and so I chose the chintz instead.) We unblocked the fireplace and surrounded it with a very pretty marble mantelpiece which I had taken from my previous house. My decorator then designed

Lady Annabel Goldsmith with her two youngest children.

the four-poster bed, using the large bed from Pelham Cottage as the base, and repeating the same flowery material to cover the walls. He cut the curtains around the bed in a particularly unusual way to resemble petals, and this gives a very pretty and romantic look. I then covered the bed with cushions. I managed to place most of my old furniture from the drawing room in Kensington in the bedroom here, such as a large and very comfortable sofa, big bedside tables covered with the same chintz, and endless bits and pieces which I had collected over the years.

The four long Queen Anne windows have the same shaped curtains as the four-poster bed, and they are also finished around the edges with that curious petal cut. I added the day-bed which I find I never use, although the dogs and cats love it. I found a very pretty black lacquer cupboard at Geoffrey Bennison's antique shop and a black lacquer chest of drawers and then, gradually, the room began to take shape.

There was already a bathroom leading off the bedroom, but we decided to extend it and add cupboards, thus making it into a bathroom-dressing room. We put in a large marble bath and a very attractive wash-basin, and I covered the walls with photographs. Now, I felt completely at home in my new bedroom. I had lived with most of the furniture for over twenty years, and also most of the pictures, and I felt rather as if I had moved the whole of Pelham Cottage into one room. Within weeks of moving in, the bedroom became, and still is, the most important room in Ormeley Lodge. I actually like to lie down: I do not like sitting down and I prefer to flop, leaning on one elbow, so this turns out to be the only room I can really lounge around in.

My three younger children, aged eleven, ten and four, have all at one time or another slept in the bed, and two of them do their homework on the sofa by the fire. Even Jimmy does most of his work in bed. When he is in England my bedroom turns into his office, where he sits scribbling away, yelling down the telephone, glaring at anyone who comes in and refusing to be budged out of bed before lunchtime. It takes me a good hour of coaxing, hinting and fighting my way through the cigar fumes finally to get him up, sighing heavily and shuffling into his dressing room. His ultimate crime is to creep into my bathroom and sit reading the *Financial Times* and puffing away at one of his endless cigars.

There is no question that my bedroom is a winner, because it adapts to the seasons. In summer, the sun pours through the windows and I have a wonderful view of the garden and across it the golf course, and on the other side it faces Ham Common with the sight and sound of horses having their morning exercise. I cannot see any other houses from my window. I am surrounded by woodland and greenery. I could be in any country house in any part of England, and yet I am between Richmond Park and Ham Common, only fifteen minutes from London.

In the winter, however cold and bleak the weather is outside, I can light the fire and within minutes the room glows with warmth and happiness, and as I know from my childhood in Ireland, there is nothing to compare with falling asleep in a room flickering with firelight.

LAURA BEAR

Laura Bear was a deputy Head Girl of St Paul's School in London and, after spending a year working in Canada, she is now an undergraduate at New Hall College, Cambridge, reading Archaeology and Anthropology. Her family home is a late 1970s house in west London.

Order is ordinary. Regularity suggests factory production lines and chickens cooped at optimum temperatures. The stars of our times, like the stars of Spielberg box-office hits, are none other than those agents of disorder, gremlins. Everything that evades the mundaneness of mass production has a cachet: customised cars, original paintings, individual style. Irregularity seems to glitter with glamour. Why then are we content with wallpapers that repeat motifs? Wallpaper music is censured, so why do we put up with wallpaper itself, not to mention matching curtains, cushions and lampshades? Why blanket the individuality of a room or uneven walls?

The acute-angled corner in my cheese-wedge-shaped bedroom could have been a source of despair, but those Laurel-and-Hardy slapstick struggles to fix sticky rectangles of paper to imperfect, sagging walls need not take place. I could have wrestled with bulging wallpaper for the Conveyor Belt Trophy (awarded to the most relentlessly regular room), but instead I create the gremlins and watch them work. With picture frames askew and tumbling into it, and filled with a precarious pile of books, the corner becomes a delicious defect. The curves of rebellious wallpaper are transformed into glittering arcs of netting which are attached over the top of pictures, and which even succeed in creeping over the ceiling, splaying shadows on the smoother white behind. Pipe lagging pulled from its functional context is sprayed with gold paint and hangs

A whirling arrangement against the white walls of a small, angular room. Two shiny cushions act as the bedhead to a mattress on the floor, and in the absence of a bedside table the lamp is hooked onto an empty picture frame. The plastic chandelier comes from a chain store. Lengths of net, in black, bronze and gold, are pinned to the window frame instead of curtains or blinds.

like matted seaweed thrown up by a storm. Debris becomes decoration, and order is ousted.

Chemistry charts in a meticulous, ordered progression the reactions between substances and has as its Bible the systematic periodic table. Chemical changes are recorded under the headings of method, results and conclusions. However, these very processes of change will often only occur if the disorder or entropy of the reactants increases as a result of the reaction. Embodied in chemistry, and conceived of as an ordered system, is the concept that reactions in the universe proceed to produce more disorder. Disorder determines whether our bread rises or our wallpaper glue sticks. To acknowledge disorder as an important factor in design accentuates its value as an impetus. The rigid framework of chemistry can contain disorder, and the rigid expectations and requirements we have of rooms could also absorb it.

The tumults and confusion in my room are an attempt to make myself realise the importance and delight of disorder. A test tube rolls on a bookcase, and a Victorian encyclopaedia of science is sandwiched in a toppling heap. These scientists' tools are on the verge of creating the disorder they are used to explore. A print of an eighteenth-century gentleman being presented with a knighthood for his services to the law and order of Britain is stranded on top of a pile of books, at the apex of the shapes whirling from wall to ceiling; eighteenth-century concepts of order and harmony are isolated in an onrush of chaos. I sympathise with the poor gentleman when I wake up in the middle of the night and don't know whether I'm still dreaming a scenario from a disaster nightmare. Disorder is dangerous and unsettling as well as challenging. A recent newspaper report of a man who murdered his wife and then shot himself described their house as full of niggling mini-malfunctions, such as taps fitted so that you scraped your hand against the wall as you turned them, doors whose bolts stuck and drawers which jammed. Domestic dramas originate in trivia, and disorder can create frustrations. My solution, when these thoughts creep into my mind as I lie in the dead of night surrounded by crooked and empty picture frames, is to remember that the gap between order and disorder is not as wide as we usually think.

In the swirl solid, formal photographs hang in rows. My great-great-grandfather sits enormous with a tiny rose and his wife fading beside him, and my grandparents smiling at their engagement with the sun creasing the blanket strung up as a backdrop. How did they choose their props? Was their choice as haphazardly spontaneous as my exploitation of hardware stores and my collection of frames culled from skips? At the turn of the century, photographic studios kept a selection of columns for aspiring Grecian maidens, woodscenes for nymphs and sturdy chairs for long exposures. The hotchpotch of fantasy, practicality and technology only became whole and seamless in the final pictures, like those in my room. It was only while the photographs of my bedroom were being taken and I was thinking about this piece that reasons for the design of my room surfaced. Disorder became ordered and, surprisingly, I found patterns among the hoarded scraps. The formulae of physics, which belong to a

Laura Bear, raider of skips and bargain basements, surveys her unstable collection.

Tight corners of an asymmetrical arrangement, with books piled in dotty disarray and objects ready to topple. Draped garden netting and other objects around the room glisten with a coating of gold or bronze spray paint.

self-referencing ordered universe, are used to determine the structure of bridges and to overcome the problems of a disordered reality. If I repeat this often enough in the middle of the night I soon fall soundly asleep, although whether this is a result of contentment or boredom I'm never sure.

Congo Curios, Smurfette's Lucky Ducky, Great Whale of China, Charge of the Knight Brigade, Flavoury Fried Vegetables and Sherwood Florist are all within easy walking distance as I write this piece in Toronto, Canada. From the world-embracing culture of cartoons comes Toronto's condensed all-nations-in-one city state of 'Wonderland'. The buildings, although all constructed from the same materials at the same time, succeed in suggesting mediaeval Britain, Imperial Japan and the Flintstones' home town of Bedrock. Design is used by the architects as a device to trigger specific associations in the shortest amount of time. The result is an exaggeration, a bloated caricature, efficient and exhilaratingly exploitative. In my room, the ridiculously huge rosary hung over a gilded mirror, the pattern from a Victorian stencil made to imitate mediaeval decorations, and an imitation Regency chandelier are my attempts to explore this type of design. A bedroom is for dreaming in, and the commercial alchemists of the imagination should know best how to whip up dreams through design. I want to dream about chapels and cypresses and to sleepwalk through the plots of Stendhal's *The Red and the Black* and Lewis's *The Monk*. The cross from Santiago de Compostela triggers a memory of the fireworks festival held yearly in front of the cathedral there. The cathedral, a Baroque secretion of gargoyles, angels and ivy, is by turns wrecked underwater, swallowed by a sheet of lava and scratched by ice as the explosions flash green, orange and grey-blue. At night the combination of the shadows from the netting around my bed, the fleur-de-lys, the tinkling chandelier and the clouds and trees through the yellow gauze shading the window make me imagine that I am a stony-eyed tomb figure in Santiago cathedral waiting to be dazzled by the fireworks. My dreams, and 'Wonderland', are thriving. Simulated, stimulating design can add anything you like to your dreams.

TESSA REAY

Tessa Reay is the younger daughter of Lord Lovat and grew up in the north of Scotland. She was a co-founder of C.C.P., a successful North Sea oil exploration company, and was the London editor of an American newspaper. At present she serves as a councillor for the Royal Borough of Kensington and Chelsea, and as a freelance journalist is an occasional contributor to various magazines. She lives in a nineteenth-century house in London with her children, Aeneas Master of Reay, her teenage daughter Laura, and her younger son Ned.

Had I been asked to find the perfect bedroom I think I would have chosen Thomas Jefferson's room at Monticello. Jefferson, an accomplished architect, designed his bedroom as two rooms – a study and a dressing room – with his four-poster placed strategically between the two. If he woke in the night he could get out of bed to the left and sit reading by the fire in his study. When he wished to dress, he would get out of his bed to the right and dress by the fire in his bedroom. The room therefore combined a number of desirable elements. Architecturally it was pleasing and the concept interesting, whilst it was also functional and attractively decorated. Had it belonged to a woman, it could have been pretty as well.

Such objectives are clearly difficult to achieve in your average London bedroom, but it is amazing what can be done with even the most unpromising material. My bedroom is in reality a minor architectural disaster, whose demerits I have carefully disguised by covering the walls, curtains and bed with a beautiful green and yellow flowery French linen called 'Les Vases'. In this way a small yellow box with funny windows is transformed into a woodland full of golden sun. In the summer when the trees in the street are in full leaf and almost brush the windows, you

A dark, secluded and inviting bedroom, whose decoration suggests the calm and privacy of a woodland glade. The bedcover and pillowcases, in white cotton inset and bordered with lace, are Victorian.

An eighteenth-century mirror
reflects the sunburst pleating in
the canopy over the bed. The
ornaments on the Biedermeier
commode include a stuffed cobra
and a pair of black and white
porcelain peahens.

cannot tell which is chintz and which is greenery as you lie and listen to the pigeon which persists in nesting on the balcony every year. In the winter when the leaves have fallen, my friends in the yellow house opposite are able to enjoy uninterrupted views of the room's more innocent activities.

Though small, my room does manage to be functional, with a useful upright desk in a recess by the window and a mass of books on shelves in another recess. Here I also keep books written or given by friends, and my favourite, my father's autobiography. At the desk, amongst other things, I used to write my diary, a habit of many years and a hazardous one, as any real diarist knows. I tried unsuccessfully to remember to keep the desk locked, until one day – and after a couple of friendships had been dislocated by my indiscretions – I found my son Aeneas reading intently in the corner of my room. He did not raise his head as I moved absent-mindedly about. Suddenly, I heard a gasp: 'Gosh, Mum, GOSH. . .' After that, I gave up writing for a time. Now I no longer try to hide it, write it less often and leave it lying around. No-one bothers to read it much any more.

It appears that reading something unpleasant in a diary seems much more poignant and real, and affects people more dramatically, than the spoken word. It was partly Tolstoy's insistence on Sonia reading all his most private diaries even before she was married to him which so shattered her confidence and contributed to the gradual disintegration of the marriage.

I came down to London from Scotland to seek my fortune in the traditional way at the beginning of the Sixties, and as I was a youthful victim of primogeniture I brought with me no furniture from my old home. But I was lucky. As the years rolled by and my fortunes changed, antiques were still reasonably cheap, and all the furniture in the room apart from the bed is Biedermeier bought for almost nothing around the Portobello Road. It is the right size for the room, simple in design and made of honey-coloured maple and cherry.

I have never suffered from the need to use a decorator, because I have strong ideas of my own, and it made me deeply unhappy when my former husband, who minded as much about his surroundings as I do, insisted for a time that we should. Perhaps this had something to do with the fact that initially my rustic Highland eye, more familiar with stags' horns and tartan, found it difficult to adjust to the more delicate requirements of London rooms. When I finally acquired a staircase I painted it shiny dark brown, so that it should resemble as closely as possible the pitch pine of a Scottish lodge. The drawing room was dark purple, but the bedroom was the same as it is now.

Against the intricately designed green and yellow of the walls of the bedroom hang a watercolour of fishermen on the Mares Pool of the Beauly River found in Putney, a small oil of the Sound of Sleat and a portrait of Mr Hope. In the nineteenth century Mr Hope gave his name to the Hope Diamond, which he owned along with a vast collection of stones. He founded the Flemish Hope Bank and to celebrate his successes had himself painted, not in the traditional pompous way, but in his

nightshirt and nightcap shaving at his window, with his shaving mirror propped up against a rose bush, and a wicked glint in his eye. There are some Tissot engravings of Mrs Newton looking like my grandmother, my favourite picture of a big Scotsman in a rowing boat with a beautiful girl tucked under either arm bearing the legend 'How happy I could be with either t'were other dear charmer away', and a precious photograph of Aeneas and Laura clutching each other and looking rather forlorn.

My bedroom is pretty but not excessively feminine, something incidentally that I suspect English men find rather distasteful. Few men can enjoy lying with only nose and eyes appearing out of a mass of frills and bows and curtains and cushions, looking for all the world like a prize bull bedecked for market. This irritation with femininity reminds me of the story of the late Lord Mowbray and Stourton whose wife Lady Mowbray sought a legal separation in the late 1950s on the grounds that he had become too dangerous to live with. It transpired in court that one of the main reasons for his extreme fury and consequent violence towards her (it was rumoured he had tried to strangle her in a lay-by) was that she used 'couvre-linges' in the bedroom. 'Couvre-linges' are pretty little frilled and embroidered pieces of silk or other material, used by Victorian ladies to cover their underclothes once they had removed them.

In any event I have no 'couvre-linges', no dressing table, no jars of make-up, no frills and furbelows, but the sheets of the bed are embroidered linen bought in salerooms and the pillows are down – not eighteen, like Caruso is said to have had on his bed, but six for mine.

Yet every bedroom should have its secrets, and to my mind the more the merrier. For example, the Chinese used the Ai-shan pillow filled with special herbal concoctions which they believed cured all manner of ailments or diseases, and what is more could cause white hair to turn black, restore lost teeth and inspire sweet dreams. But I prefer the more exotic fancy of the Renaissance ladies, who favoured black satin sheets better to show the whiteness of their skins. Nowadays such delicacies are, sadly, almost unobtainable, thanks to our twentieth-century obsession with sun-tanned skin.

Like Jefferson, I am the proud possessor of a beautiful eighteenth-century four-poster, which I bought for one hundred pounds as a result of the throw of a dice nearly twenty years ago, but unlike his mine takes pride of place bang in the middle of the bedroom. It is narrowish for a double bed, but the initial investment of a luxurious mattress has paid off.

It is easy to forget that daily trauma of the bedroom – actually getting out of bed. The world must divide into two on this subject, those who do mind and those who do not, though age may have something to do with it. There is a theory in my house that 'great' people are never up before eleven o'clock – in which case my children are clearly destined for fame and fortune, whereas I am resigned to mediocrity.

My former husband Hugh fell into the first of these categories. He found it difficult to get to sleep, but once asleep found it harder to wake. On one occasion he invited friends to shoot at his castle in Holland. In the late autumn, the wild duck fly in from the Rhine marshes at dawn to feed

A Biedermeier secretaire stands in a corner by the window. The same chintz has been used for the curtains, the wall coverings and the hangings of the four-poster bed.

with the domestic and ornamental birds on the moat surrounding the old brick walls of the seventeenth-century house. In the cold frosty first light, each guest was in his appointed place waiting for the duck to come skimming over the trees, all except their host Hugh, who was still nowhere to be seen. Soon a brace of duck came in high, circling the moat, and at that moment one of the heavy shutters of Hugh's bedroom slowly pushed open and the barrel of a shotgun held by pyjama'd arms nosed its way out. Bang, and again, bang. A right and left. Then the arms and gun retreated, the shutter closed firmly, and the guests were left to carry on.

Though the comfort of my bed is great I am fortunate indeed in finding the leaving of it fairly tolerable, but as a seventeenth-century poet wrote:

In bed we laugh, in bed we cry,

And born in bed, in bed we die.

In my bed there has been a great deal of laughing and a fair amount of crying. But because of the caution of modern science, none of my children was born in it. Nevertheless, each of the three has put in a request for it, either right away or as soon as possible, or even when I am dead. My mother had six children in her great big bed at Beaufort, though the last was born in Edinburgh. I can remember her dragging the great big cardboard box which held the necessary paraphernalia down the wooden passage to her bedroom when the time came, and the whole house would be hushed for hours. We would go off into the woods and wait.

In those days having a baby was still rather secret and it was thought indelicate to talk about it. When Aunt Sybil Fraser was expecting her son Simon she told the other children only that the family was going to get something 'New and Wonderful Quite Soon'. When the baby finally arrived, his little brother Ian Fraser screamed and threw a tantrum, because he thought the something 'New and Wonderful' was going to be a brand new green motor car and not a dreary baby.

To my knowledge no-one has recently died in my bed. Perhaps I shall: in which case my good luck will have held. I can see myself lying pale and exhausted against huge feather pillows, a small smile playing on my fevered lips and the TV remote control firmly gripped under the bedclothes. To take it all too seriously, as did David Copperfield's Dora, child-wife or not, means you end up as one of literature's most tedious heroines. And that is something to be avoided at all costs.

SARAH FORBES

Sarah Forbes and her husband, actor John Standing, live in a nineteenth-century studio in Highgate. Sarah is the eldest daughter of actress Nanette Newman and film director and writer Bryan Forbes. Her book of poetry, I Thought We Were Friends, *was published after she left school; she then travelled in America before joining the staff of a women's magazine and later becoming a freelance journalist.*

I had always been under the arrogant assumption that most single men's bedrooms were sexual transit lounges, a place for lonely hearts to rest their weary bones before catching their on-going flights.

John Standing's was different. For a start it was wall-papered pink, which immediately crushed any preconceived ideas I had harboured about bachelor hunting grounds; secondly, his sheets were so pathetically frayed that I fell in love with him and the room simultaneously.

Apart from being pink, the room was fairly masculine, dominated by a huge, dark, double chest of drawers that had belonged to his great-grandfather and a dubious-looking commode upon which his grandmother once sat. As he already had these two monuments, which like myself looked like remaining permanent fixtures, I set about feminising the rest of the room.

The first thing that had to go was the bed itself. It had obviously seen better days, not to mention nights, and we replaced it with a hand-made six-foot bed, the arrival of which happily coincided with a trip to New York, so that I was able to raid Bloomingdale's linen department for non-iron sheets and valances. I have always had a passion for American and English quilts and have a collection of over twenty, so I'm constantly changing the look of the room. In the summer I love the room to reflect a feeling of light and coolness, so I usually try to keep everything very white and crisp-looking; in the winter I pile on heavier quilts and leave another folded at the foot of the bed to use as a buffer against the cold greyness of the weather outside.

Living in a three-roomed studio forces you to use each room for several different purposes. Our bedroom is really just an extension of our sitting room, which in turn is an extension of the kitchen. If we're alone, we sometimes eat dinner in bed, we always watch television sprawled across the bed; in fact, we probably spend less time sleeping than we do just *living* in the bedroom.

I am a complete bookaholic, and there are always too many books and too little space. I changed John's original tiny bedside tables for two vast coffee tables, and my side is cluttered with sentimental memorabilia: boxes filled with old letters, packets of photographs, a silver glass bought

A corner of the room with a pink painted doll's house from Sarah's childhood and a pair of sailor teddy bear slippers.

A view into the bedroom from the sitting room of the studio, where John Standing's painting is in progress.

on our honeymoon, my journals (written every night in bed), favourite books and magazines as well as vitamins, chewing gum and all the other junk one accumulates. John's side is much more practical. His houses the telephone, the television controls and the odd script, but its main purpose is as a grave-yard for the contents of his pockets. In the same way as I feel sentimental about love-letters and their close proximity, John treasures old theatre tickets, week-old newspapers, used Kleenex and redundant foreign currency.

When I arrived there were no curtains; one of the windows was shuttered and the other had a sort of fake Gucci blind left by a previous owner. One day when John was out filming, in a rare moment of inspiration, I rushed down the road to a marvellous shop called Lunn Antiques and bought a pair of lacy Victorian tablecloths. Armed with a staple-gun and steely nerves I wavered at the top of a ten-foot ladder, trying to create what I hoped was a romantic effect. I hung a very thin Japanese paper blind behind the billowing curtains, so that at night the light filters through the web of lace, staining the ceiling with shadows. In the summer I leave the shutters of the other window open, and some nights we can lie beneath the punka fan and see the moon high above the Parisian-type rooftops.

Our bedroom looks out onto a courtyard, around which the studios are grouped. Light is of prime importance here, and I managed almost to double the light in this room by finding a large mirror which exactly fits behind the bed. The only disadvantage of having a mirror as a head-rest is that you are forced to check your state of health the moment you open your eyes, but usually it's only fatigue that has set in overnight, not leprosy.

My favourite painting in the bedroom is the large Victorian watercolour hanging opposite the door. It's by an artist called A. Wilde Parsons and John found it in a junk shop in Marlborough for seventy pounds. It's of two people shrimping by the English seaside and to me, it's evocative of childhood summers. I also love the watercolour beside my bed, which John gave me last Christmas. He had painted an interior of our sitting room without my knowing. It has a wonderful faded, washed-out quality about it.

I'm sure the overall impression of the room is one of complete clutter and chaos, but I do my best to avoid this. The times I become the most passionate about the bedroom are when I see it captured in photographs, looking just as I imagine it in my mind's eye — tidy, romantic and unruffled. The stark reality of dirty socks and crumpled sheets is lost behind the camera's ability to freeze and record a moment in time.

Sarah Forbes at the typewriter in her yellow-walled kitchen/dining room.

THE DUCHESS OF BEAUFORT

The Duchess of Beaufort and her husband live at the Dower House at Badminton in Gloucestershire. They will soon be moving to Badminton House itself, as the Duke of Beaufort recently succeeded to the title.

Sometimes, when I lie awake at night, worrying myself stiff over some totally unimportant matter, I just *hate* my bedroom. I long for the time to come when I can get out of my crumpled sheets and face up to my problems, which I know will diminish with the coming of daylight. Luckily these times are rare. I am a good sleeper, good enough never to have possessed any sleeping pills, and what I call a bad night is being awake for a couple of hours. At any rate, I think that too much sleep is bad for me, and, at my age, six hours is ample.

The big problem of how to stop oneself worrying still remains. When my husband is not there I can always turn on the light and read, and that usually works. Sometimes, I even turn on the television and watch a video, but I have never yet seen the end of a tape. Most of the time I sleep soundly, and, I am sorry to say, sometimes snore – or so my husband tells me, but he may be exaggerating.

So it is not often that I hate my bedroom. Usually I love it. It is my refuge, particularly when the house is full of guests. I sneak away to it, knowing that I am being a bad hostess, and somewhat guiltily watch telly. Incidentally, I am a television addict. 'This programme is unwatchable,' I say, and go on watching it. It has been known for some well-meaning but tactless guest to follow me to my room in order to 'keep me company'. Furious, I have to stump downstairs again, resolving that that particular person will not be asked again in a hurry.

I have a four-poster bed which is a great joy to me. My husband gave it to me for one of my birthdays. It may be Sheraton – at any rate I choose to think that it is Sheraton. Under the canopy it has what I believe is called a sunburst, made of pleated organza gathered into a rosette in the middle. It is very wide, a full six foot in width, so that even when we are not sleeping too well my husband and I do not disturb each other – much.

Tom Parr from Colefax & Fowler did up the whole room, and very competently he did it too. We have often worked together, and I have also often worked with cheaper firms, and what a difference there is! He excels not only in the actual making-up of the curtains and so on, but also in his knowledge of proportion and design. I always know what I want. Indeed, I am opinionated and positively pig-headed and, alas, sometimes wrong. But with Tom, all I have to do is to choose the stuff, choose the colour, perhaps make a rough sketch of the type of pelmet, and all the rest is done for me, exactly as I want it.

After the basic decoration was finished I then set about mucking the room up. I don't do this intentionally, it just happens. Indeed, I have to be careful to stop it from bordering on the squalid. Books pile up beside the bed, china ornaments clutter the place up. Many of the latter are not particularly nice, being presents from the children and past servants – but once given to me, they become mine and I love them. Besides, one must always remember that good taste must never override good manners.

My clothes cupboards would be considered adequate for any normal person, but I am not normal. I am a hoarder. I keep clothes that I have been fond of and am now far too fat for, in the pathetic hope that some miracle will happen and I will be able to slide into them once again. Even if I did manage to do so, they are so out of date that no-one would want to be seen dead in them.

Looking-glasses I hate these days. I have two in my room. The one on the dressing-table is copied from the Zoffany painting of Queen Charlotte in the Royal Collection, and is swathed in spotted muslin. The other, a cheval glass, I dearly hate. It makes me look much fatter than I am, but possibly this idea of mine is open to argument.

I like the idea of myself looking fluffily romantic amidst my pillows, wearing a lace negligée and delicately lit by a shaded lamp. In fact, I am usually looking somewhat down-to-earth, wearing a nightdress which even the village jumble sale would not be happy to accept, and reading a book under a practical and piercing little modern lamp – which, as the years go by, seems to be getting less piercing, just as the print of the books seems to be getting smaller. What a bore it is to be getting older.

On the other hand, was it so much fun being a child? Particularly, at bedtime? How horrid it was, being put to bed so early: off one went at six-thirty, with strict instructions to go to sleep, and half an hour later Nanny would come back and demand to know why one wasn't asleep. I was always longing for the night to be over in those days. And there were the nightmares. Nowadays, I do sometimes have anxious dreams which I am glad to wake up from, but when I was a child I was constantly being chased by wolves.

My own children used to be brought to see me every morning while I

The draping of the dressing-table mirror was inspired by a painting by Zoffany in the Royal Collection. The curtains at the window are buff linen.

The Duchess of Beaufort in her garden.

The fireplace to the right of the bed, with four prints of Badminton house discovered in the attics there.

was still in bed. It was only a moderate pleasure on both sides: 'Darling, please don't touch that'; 'No, you cannot go back to Nanny yet, she doesn't want you till nine o'clock'; 'Now do leave my lipstick alone'. In fact it was a great relief, both to me and to the children, when Nanny came to fetch them and the invasion of my privacy was over.

Yes, I think that privacy is the dominant word for my bedroom. I do not live in it, and I certainly do not entertain in it, but I do escape into it. It is not the most important room in my life. Proper life goes on downstairs, or in the garden.

Within the next few months I shall be leaving this house and garden in order to move into Badminton House. My feelings are divided, for there is a deep sadness, particularly about leaving the garden, but also great excitement. What will my new bedroom be like? It is one of the few rooms we will re-decorate. I feel strongly that every newcomer to an old house should only be allowed to re-decorate one, or perhaps two rooms. What is good taste to one generation seems to be vandalism to the next. My bedroom is going to be the room in which Queen Mary slept throughout the War. She had it painted a cold pea-soup colour, to go with peach satin hangings. This is certainly not to my taste, but maybe I ought to learn to live with it. However, I am not going to. Tom Parr will be called in, and once again I will be opinionated and pig-headed, and once again I am sure he will succeed in making me very pleased with the result. But think how many sleepless hours I am going to have, worrying about the whole project.

MIN HOGG

Min Hogg is the Editor-in-Chief of the international decoration magazine, The World of Interiors, *and her career in journalism spans twenty years of work on newspapers and magazines. She lives in the top-floor flat of a house in a London square.*

Decoration, good and bad, and the way people live, fascinates me and always has. 'House Freaks', I believe we are called.

I never meet anyone without speculating as to what it is like where they live, and I long to snoop. Decoration, or the lack of it, is after all *the* give-away to a person's character. The neurotically tidy, the ingenious, the flamboyant, the constipated, the feminine, the masculine, the mean, the generous and the aesthete reveal themselves, consciously or unconsciously, at home.

Once this passion for houses in all their forms was merely a hobby, but having edited *The World of Interiors* magazine from its inception in 1981, snooping has become not just respectable but part of my very full-time job. Work keeps me away from home a great deal, both at the office and on photographic forays all over the globe. While travelling, there is nothing I yearn for more than my own possessions, pictures, sheets and above all bed-springs, and the delights of returning to them know no bounds. Alas, for the time being, this pleasure cannot be indulged in.

As I write (in bed), rhythmic thuds and torrents of rubble falling from above are a painful reminder that my dear old bedroom pictured here, the very pivot of my domestic life, no longer exists. The friendly cracks in the ceiling, pink walls sooty from an open fire and peeling paint – of which I was inordinately fond – are undergoing major surgery. Having stored all the furniture, and temporarily camping out in a rented flat on a lower floor, I have watched stricken as the skip outside in the street fills up with my walls, my mangled cornices and the entire roof. Rehabilitation from this operation – my own and the flat's – cannot be expected for some months, and I envisage a prolonged spell of intensive care after the workmen leave, pulling and pushing it back into familiar shape, before I can even begin to resume the intimate relationship I absolutely count on between myself and my bedroom.

As far as sleeping quarters are concerned, I have always been rather lucky. Though I was supposed to have been delivered in the soulless confines of a London hospital, my birth actually took place prematurely in a very pretty spare room of the country house belonging to an aunt and uncle, where my mother had dashed after a morning's househunting in the neighbourhood, to produce me in time for an early tea.

Since that day goodish space and sympathetic architecture have always been mine to play with, decoratively speaking. Never have I been faced with having to disguise the unpleasing proportions of a metal-framed Crittal window, nor been lumbered with a wall of flush-fronted-hanging-cupboards-incorporating-vanitory-unit-complete-with-fluorescent-strip.

My first bedroom was the nursery of my parents' house in Regent's Park where, as the youngest, I inevitably became marooned, and although I had it all to myself the lino floor and toy cupboards concealing Teddy and Shirley Temple the doll – who were by then undergoing a period of disfavour – never quite let me forget that it *was* the nursery.

In a reshuffle I finally graduated to my very own room with no childish connotations, and for the first time was in charge of the decorations. My mother and I mastered the art of wallpapering the hard way. A vine-leaf trellis in greens on white, bird's-egg blue ceiling and curtain stuff, together with a small Regency faux-bamboo four-poster were very *à la mode*, I thought, and with windows on two sides I could see that immense stretch of green, The Dogs' Paradise in the Park, and in the stillness of summer nights could hear lions roaring at the Zoo.

Evidence of my chronic capacity to clutter things up soon came to light. On becoming an art student at London's Central School, prophetically studying Interior Design, I injected a draughtsman's table, portfolios, projects, junk-shop finds, dress-making equipment, together with my entire wardrobe strewn on the floor, and created an entirely different ambience. I adored the chaos, and was thankful that parental monitoring was kept in check by the five floors to be climbed in order to reach me.

In the next general post at the family house I was awarded a really large room with bath en suite in a kind of side wing, and for the first time tasted the joys of almost total privacy. The room was big enough for a huge bed, a piano, bookcases, chairs, a sofa, a dressing-table and on occasion the ping-pong table too. I could smuggle people in and out with the greatest of ease. The only snag was that it had been decorated, shortly before becoming mine, with my brother in mind, and although the washed-out indigo walls and faded red and cream chintz curtains had a certain style, they were not what I would have chosen if I had been let rip.

previous pages
A warm, inviting bedroom in tones of pink and saffron. Over the bed hang fifteen coloured engravings of the British Army in Burma, dominated by a saffron silk ribbon tied in a bow. The headboard is covered in pink and white Indian printed cotton, the pink and white quilt was brought home from a trip to Jaipur, and the same colours are used in the scallop-edged sheets and pillowcases.

Min Hogg working in bed.

One cannot live at home for ever, and it was a chance meeting with the curate of St Anne's, Soho, that lead me into realising a vague ambition of getting a flat in that parish. One of the congregation was leaving for calmer pastures in Brighton, and I took over her two floors of a mid-Georgian house in Rupert Street. Here for the first time in my life I had to contend with a nice but small bedroom, whose size and location precluded it from becoming the all-purpose room I had invariably managed before.

I treated it to the unorthodox combination of a large-scale Art Nouveau wallpaper in sickly greens and marmalade with curtains of pink sprigged white cotton (pre-Laura Ashley). Much to my outrage the man who came to mend my sash cord thought I was doing up a hairdressing salon. I spent eleven years in that flat, and the bedroom was never redecorated. Soho grime soon mellowed the wallpaper, and its dark cocoon-like quality suited my Sixties' life of work, by then at *The Observer* on the home pages, followed by cinema, parties and night clubs.

I might have been there to this day had not a Chinese restaurant opened beneath, treating me not only to the permanent aroma of monosodium glutamate *à l'ail*, but – much, much worse – to the infinite terror of marauding rats. So, from the ridiculous to the sublime, and I have been for the past ten years a resident of that 'secluded garden square' within spitting distance of Harrods so beloved of estate agents.

Life has turned another full circle. Here I am back on the top floor, though with a lift this time, and there is a distinct nursery feeling about my low-ceilinged rooms, but, thank God, my bedroom is once again the centre of the action. A somewhat countryfied air pervades this flat, and for a time before the move I toyed with the idea of using as my decorative inspiration what strikes me as the definitive cottage bedroom in F. W. Ellwell's poignant painting 'The First Born'.

However, procrastination being second nature to me, I found myself with only just over a week in which to do up the whole place. Possessing no half-tester bed, no rose chintz, no suitable ottoman or rush-seated chair – let alone a fresh-faced young father by my side, as in Ellwell's picture – I had no alternative but to plump for three nice pinks on the Dulux chart.

The walls were painted one shade, the ceiling another, woodwork and doors a combination of all three. Although in no time the subtleties of my three-toned room had merged into what looked like a single colour, I have never regretted that pink. Good by day and, with shiny pink card lampshades, good by night, I should find it hard to improve upon, especially in east-facing rooms reflecting the massed greens of a London square.

Next came the log fire (a pretty fireplace was already there). First it was the real thing, but humping wood became such a bore that I capitulated to the gas variety, and it could not be better. I have encouraged dust and small falls of mortar from the chimney to accumulate, I have broken and muddled up the logs so now its dancing flames, charred logs, heaps of ash and orange embers fool everyone. The dressing-table is a long wallpaperer's trestle from Gamages with the legs shortened and with a gathered skirt to the ground in a red and white striped sari cotton, made up by my mother.

For the rest, it just arrived by degrees. More and more pictures have well-nigh obliterated the walls, a nice blonde-wood knee-hole desk supports the typewriter, which is shrouded in a shocking-pink cotton damask scarf when lying fallow, and a wonderfully engineered telescoping three-tiered dumb waiter holds the television and lots of books on my side of the bed.

I often change the covering of the headboard. It is only a piece of printed cotton pinned on, and there are drawers full of alternatives to choose from. The same thing goes for the quilted cover – I seem to have accumulated textiles by the dozen. Dinner, on staying-at-home nights, is

The dressing-table is a wall-paperer's trestle skirted in striped sari cotton.

invariably in bed. I've never seen the point of dressing again after a bath and dirtying a whole lot more clothes, so it's straight into my faithful blue towelling bathrobe and to bed for the rest of the evening. I have television, telephone to hand, a drink, the newspapers, magazines and books, and if I have an article to write that gets done there too, as the concentration needed is quite out of the question in the hullabaloo of my office. Thus settled in, it is also perfectly possible to entertain. Guests first sit with drinks beside the blazing fire and then pull their chairs up to the bed and join us for dinner spread out on the somewhat unsteady surface. There has been the occasional complaint, not to mention a few spills, but on the whole it is rather a lark. When the present building work is finished and I can return home, far from branching out into a spanking new kind of decoration, I expect I shall put it all back exactly as it was.

Above the chimney piece hangs a portrait of 'some old Hogg – I don't know who'. Min Hogg's favourite bedroom, in a painting by F. W. Ellwell, is second from the left in the portrait frame. Around the portrait a collection of pictures includes a photo of Min's grandfather in India and a drawing of Lady Diana Cooper, aged sixteen, done by her mother. Below stands a line of pear-shaped objects and African lacquer boxes.

ZANDRA RHODES

Zandra Rhodes is one of Britain's best-known designers, and her talents range from the creation of ballgowns to designs for bed linen. She graduated from The Royal College of Art in the 1960s and started her dress designing career three years later with the opening of The Fulham Road Clothes Shop in London. Now Zandra Rhodes has an international clientele. Ten years ago she bought a dilapidated Victorian house in North Kensington where she lives today.

At a certain point in your life you can either sit back and accept your surroundings as they are, or you can decide to make them beautiful, an extension of yourself. I have done the latter. I feel as close to my surroundings as a tortoise does to its shell.

The prime example of this is my bedroom, which portrays a world I am always close to: the world of fantasy. This is an essential element to me. It is part of my business. The walls and ceilings of my bedroom are covered in ruched tulle in my own special print over gold lamé, with concealed pink mirrors that throw out a wondrous pink glow to help my mood. A gold silk-satin printed bedspread lies on my circular bed, and luxurious cushions abound. The feeling of a fabulous sheikh's abode is no accident. The curved bedside table, which is a little longer and wider than a bedside table needs to be, houses treasured mementos, and the whole scene is guarded by one of my blackamoors.

An essential ingredient of my room is the glorious view and access to my magic garden, where I have lots of Gro-lites to look after my plants. Looking out onto all this gives me endless pleasure, a feeling of calmness to help me rest and concentrate while I am relaxing in bed and sketching out new ideas. If there is something special I wish to see on television I

The low, circular tented bed in this circular room has cushions covered in Painted Lady satins, some of which are finished with a gold frill. Mirror and reflective foil are placed behind the fabric wall coverings, to give a glittery light.

switch on my portable, which is suspended from the roof by an original chain and padlock by Andrew Logan, inset with gorgeous jewelled stones and mirrors and held in the hands of the blackamoor.

Once I actually spent a whole day in bed when I was correcting proofs for my book. Except for the incessant rain pouring onto the plants outside my window there was silence, and I was surrounded by cushions and comfort, the hours spread out beautifully before me. It was magical. Generally, I do not go to bed before one o'clock in the morning. However, sometimes I make it a little earlier and take the bed-tray with me; with the idea of reading I rest a book on it, reach for my sketch pad, and ensure that the telephone is by my side as I am often called two or three times during the night by friends from all over the world. I settle down cosily, read a couple of sentences, and the next thing I know my alarm is telling me it is time to get up – six-thirty. As usual, I have slept with all the lights on and simply fallen asleep over everything.

When I wake in summer, full daylight streams across to me, as I never close the curtains or pull the turquoise blinds because the plants at my windows love light. The Gro-lites go on automatically at six a.m. in my dressing room next door, so even in winter I have the pleasure of orchids blooming and ferns looking fantastic. The dressing room is a recently conceived extension of my bedroom, which I am coming to adore just as much. This area is a mixture of the exotic and the practical. The glorious, tiny bulbs around my dressing-room mirror switch on by remote control, and even though I am only in there for ten minutes it is a fabulous beginning to the day. As in my bedroom, my own printed fabrics are to be found everywhere, and I am near my plants once again. The practical element is my fantastic, efficient, pink wardrobe. It was built to my own personal specifications for my clothes and the hectic life I lead. The original plans were given to me by Billy Gaylord, the San Francisco designer.

Although, as I have said, the total concept of the bedroom is one of fantasy, the look of glamorous extravaganza was achieved in a very down-to-earth way.

My bed has to be circular and it has to be in this position, because the room is so small that you would hurt your leg on the corner of a square bed when coming in through the door. The idea when I came here was to convert every floor into potentially self-contained apartments, because this would increase the value of the house. My bedroom was small and square, and, by taking off one corner, I was able to create a bathroom out of the wine cellar on the other side of the wall. The walls themselves were an even more basic problem, because they were in such a bad condition that it was a case of either plastering them or leaving them bare; so the easy answer in here was to tent the bare brick walls with fabric, and some of the tulle left over from making a collection of ballgowns was used for this purpose. Many of the solutions are artistic, but they are also practical.

I am surrounded by pictures of myself in the bedroom at the moment, but this is by accident. I love picture frames and once they contained photographs of all my friends which I kept around my bed. During the

Zandra Rhodes, photographed by Robyn Beeche.

The dark, glittering bathroom, converted from a wine cellar, has china fan shades by Carol McNicholl, squiggle motif tiles and a shell-shaped hand-basin, all continuing the design themes in the bedroom next door.

process of putting together my book, my friends' pictures were raided from the frames for the pages of the book, and I filled the empty spaces with pictures of myself. I simply have not had the chance to reorganise everything.

Friends used to tell me they found it disconcerting that I lived in one big design, but it is not disconcerting to me: it is very important. I do become concerned that I might be over-precious about my surroundings, but I love having friends to share them with. For years now my house has been like a private hotel, with all my most wonderful friends passing through. The most refreshing time in my house, and for my friendships, is when some of the crowd are here. We feel like a big family, and because we all have our own special involvements we sit around and talk about our work. Barbara Nessim, a computer artist who has been a great influence on my work, stays often, and so does Divine, the female impersonator, when he is in London. I give dinner parties for everyone on Saturdays.

When I get myself sufficiently disciplined to do exercises for my back, I walk through to the dressing room at night and lie on the floor in complete darkness, except for the garden lights which filter through the greenery. Peacefulness surrounds me there. My garden is my greatest joy, and from my bed I can see across to its different levels with mirror mosaic inset into the walls, garlands of shells, a polystyrene statue of a Mexican god called a chakmul, and my white plants, all of which I adore.

I can even go one step further. There is yet another stage in reaching my ultimate dream room. It will be on the uppermost floor, and it will be circular, with the walls draped in printed fabric like this room, but it will have a ceiling of glass. It will be like lying in a wonderful four-poster bed with a canopy of stars, and I will be able to look straight up into the sky. There will be a balcony filled with white camellias, and I shall have a bird's-eye view of my garden. This bedroom will surpass all those that have gone before it. It will be a room at the top.

An exotic chain designed by Andrew Logan, and held by a blackamoor figure, suspends the television. The brass door handles and all the power points in the room are surrounded by a ruff of pleated gold lamé – an inventive solution to the problem of disguising the staples holding the fabrics onto the walls.

ELDRED EVANS

Eldred Evans is an architect. She qualified at the Architectural Association in the 1960s and won a scholarship to Yale University. For twenty years Eldred Evans has worked with her husband, David Shalev. They live in an apartment in a Victorian building in north London and a studio in Cornwall, and have an eight-year-old daughter, Elantha.

I have lived in this apartment, on the second floor of a white stucco Victorian building, for the past nineteen years. I have seldom wanted to move, as I am an extremely contented flat dweller. I would, in fact, feel uncomfortable living in a house with a garden, however desirable they may be. I am a city dweller. I enjoy being within ten minutes of the centre of London and walking to work. I like the density of city life – a density that can only be achieved if people live in apartments, as in other countries in Europe. The apartment is horizontal living, and it has only been realised here in the form of the mansion building. My apartment has the feeling of having been purpose-built. The reason for this is that the building is entered in the middle, not from the edges. It has a twelve-metre-square footprint, and the staircase to each level is in the middle and to one side of the plan. Each level contains one flat – further subdivisions have fortunately not taken place. I chose to live on the second floor. The quality of light is superior, and with lower ceilings the rooms have better proportions.

The plan of the apartment is organised around a central hallway which is our dining space, and in fact the centre of our daily life. It is internal, cool in summer and warm in winter. Here we read and design, Elantha does her homework and we enjoy meals with our friends. All the other rooms of the flat open directly off this space. To the north, facing onto the rear garden, are Elantha's room in which, amongst her clutter, stands the upright piano, the compact kitchen which we made ourselves, the bathroom, which is in fact a very large room, and our bedroom. Facing south onto the street is the living room, furnished with early Aalto, Corbusier and Breuer designs laid out around a hand-made Belgian rug. Next to it is our study, which is occasionally used as a guest room.

The flat is white, and on the walls hang many fine examples of the work of my father, Merlyn Evans, as well as some of our own architectural models.

I made two alterations as soon as I moved in, and none since. I opened the bedroom into the living area, and two bedrooms into another – the smaller room became a dressing room to the larger. Both these openings adjoin the outer envelope of the building. At some stage I will make more such openings, so that it will be possible to walk around the perimeter of the plan. At one glance it will be possible to comprehend the entire external enclosure. Openings of this kind accentuate depth, and unify and blur the edges between functional definitions. I prefer openness to compartmentalisation. There is also an enhanced quality of light, with deep winter sun penetrating the entire flat, another way into each space and varying vistas. It is interesting that there is more floor area here than in a three-storey town house.

The bedroom is en suite with the living area, and measures roughly six by three and a half metres. The one window faces north-east and looks onto dense greenery, which, for half the year at least, cuts off the view of the Royal Free Hospital. A holland blind covers the window and the entire wall. On early summer mornings the sun shines through the blind, creating a beautiful abstract design. David wakes regularly at seven each morning to prepare breakfast. I take my daughter to the bus at eight-fifteen, and am in the office by eight-thirty. The routine seldom varies. We are at the drawing board most of the day, and return home exhausted. The bedroom is never used during the day. Neither of us takes naps, and we are seldom ill. We do, however, spend as much time in a bedroom as at work. I have slept roughly the equivalent of sixteen years, in eight bedrooms – six of these years in this one. All of those rooms have been sparsely furnished. Initially, because I couldn't afford to furnish them; now, because I prefer an uncluttered space.

The size of a bedroom is important. Mine is just right. If they are too large they tend to be furnished like a living room, with the bed an adjunct to one side. Enormous settees, cupboards, chests and drapery are brought in but rarely used. The few objects I have are used regularly. Again, the size of the bed is important. Ours is just under two metres square and as low as possible. It is for the three of us. The frame was purpose-made, of slatted wood on casters. The mattress was made by the General Welfare Company and is very hard. There is no headboard or padding to the sides, no concealed lights or switches. There are no cupboards visible in the room and, therefore, no clothes lying around waiting to be put away. All too often, bedrooms have wall-to-wall mirror-faced cupboards which lend an anonymous feeling, like a department store or shoe shop. With no

Eldred Evans. Behind her are photographs of some of the buildings she and her husband have designed.

Opposite the bed, a large Victorian pub mirror, beneath which stand a pair of Corbusier bascalon chairs and two stools by Alvar Aalto. Reflected in the mirror is a white unit that contains space for clothes storage and divides the bedroom area from the rest of the apartment.

cupboards or radiators there are four walls to use and decorate. There is no dressing-table implying an activity. There is no television to disrupt a night's sleep. The room is a subsidiary space used mainly in artificial light. The white walls and positive colour give it a cool, refreshing atmosphere, and the only activities generated by the furnishing are reading, chatting and sleeping.

When I moved in, the bedroom was an ordinary room with a door. All I did was to open a connection to the living room just over a metre wide, letting in the low winter sun, and to construct the low cupboard unit next to the existing door. This unit gives the room its contained feeling. The mirror is from a Victorian pub that was demolished. In it I can see the reflected image of the two mezzotints, and in front of it stand two Corbusier bascalon chairs and Aalto stools. A Best and Lloyd wall lamp is fixed beside the cupboard unit, which has another mirror and two shelves. The three duvet covers and cases are all from Habitat, each colour subtly changing the mood of the room from green to red to blue. A bench unit runs the entire length of the north wall under the window.

The room is for two, and for the family at weekends. It is welcoming to all and not designed specifically to suit the needs and tastes of one member, rendering the others mere intruders or visitors. The weekends are the time when we all have breakfast in bed and enjoy an extra few moments relaxing and reading before starting the day, quite often to return to the office again. The last four years have been the hardest in our lives. As modern architects in Britain we find ourselves out on a limb, in spite of the fact that our architecture is considerate and human, two of our more successful buildings being a Home for younger physically-handicapped people and, by contrast, a precision engineering works. One of our competition wins was the design for the Taoiseach Residence and State Guest House in Phoenix Park, Dublin. As architects we are involved in space making. We are seldom interior designers. We attempt to make spaces that are flexible enough for the occupiers themselves to mould and shape to their own requirements and taste. We find in many instances that the names of spaces are unrelated to their true purpose. Frank Lloyd Wright called the kitchen a workspace. For us, our bedroom is the quiet space, for inner reflection and regeneration.

Red carnations and a child's plastic alligator on the windowsill.

Addendum by Elantha Evans

The room is square. The bed is square. The bed can also be moved into other positions. It's on wheels. Dave Hall made the bed. I helped paint it. The mattress was made by the blind.

I like the mattress because it is hard and bouncy. There is a cupboard in the room and one of my great pleasures is to hoist myself onto the top and take a flying leap onto the bed. The blind is brown and in the morning there is a yellow patch by the window. I get frightened when it is moved by the wind. It makes strange shadows.

I dash into the room to see what I look like when I'm wearing new clothes. I see myself in an enormous mirror which came from an old pub.

The room is very comfortable to be in.

Symmetrical style: over the bed hang Pentaptych Numbers 1 and 2 by Merlyn Evans, Eldred Evans' father. A Best and Lloyd lamp is attached to the wall on the left of the bed. On the shelf are pig sculptures done by Elantha Evans when she was seven. (top left) A corner of the window seat that runs the whole length of the wall to the right of the bed.

THE COUNTESS OF LICHFIELD

Lady Lichfield lives in a flat in Eaton Square, in London, and also runs Shugborough Hall, her husband's family home in the country which now belongs to the National Trust. They also have a holiday house on the island of Mustique. Lady Lichfield is a lady-in-waiting to HRH Princess Anne. She has three children, and frequently travels abroad with her husband, photographer Patrick Lichfield.

This is the first bedroom that I have felt really happy with. We have moved house six or seven times in the nine years since we married and done up two or three bedrooms, but this one has turned out just as I imagined it and wanted it to be.

The four-poster bed is totally indulgent. It is in fact an old Heal's bed which my husband had in his flat before we married, but with posts added. When we first put it in this tall room it looked much too low, like a mattress, so it was decided to dress it up in this opulent way. The room could take it as it lent itself well to this vaguely Edwardian look, which we like as it is both sophisticated and very pretty.

David Mlinaric was the natural person to ask to help in the re-decoration of this flat, as he had totally re-done the family flat at Shugborough when the family moved back there in the 1960s. Without his sense of direction and ability to make bold decisions I would have been completely at sea, and he so understood the kind of thing we wanted to do. He found the chintz, which looked rather large and daunting in a small piece, but the idea was to let the material be, and not use complicated drapes and swags. I find it pretty in the summer and cosy in the winter – a perfect combination. The ribbon wallpaper in this room is, I believe, a copy of an old one, and oddly enough when the room was

The tall, canopied four-poster bed with a Victorian cotton bed-cover has a buttoned daybed at its foot. The bed-hangings, curtains and side tables are in the same glazed, flowered chintz; the walls are covered with paper with an Edwardian trellis pattern.

finished I remembered that as a child at Hagly Hall, my mother's old home, I had slept in a room with the same paper – so it brought back pleasant memories, even though that old room was supposed to be haunted and indeed had a cupboard that creaked strangely.

I have a great love of flowers, which is why they are all around me here – on the walls, the windows and in the bits of china in the room, some of which are the Danish Flora Danica given to us by my step-father-in-law. Other pieces of china are part of a nineteenth-century washing set. They evoke the country and the traditional English look which I hoped to achieve, as I tried to keep away from that 'done-up' London smartness which I feel can sometimes be so unsympathetic, and difficult to live up to with the active family life that we have.

The flower border on the walls is followed into the passage, and this gives the continuity we wished for whereby each room should lead comfortably into the next. The bows and sprigged ribbon run into the sweetpeas outside, which in turn surround the groups of flower paintings I collected years ago when I worked in the Old Master Drawings Department at Sotheby's. In those days one could buy for a few pounds very pretty little eighteenth- and nineteenth-century botanical watercolours all in a lot – they looked and sometimes were quite tatty, but framed up they are lovely. I used to do a certain amount of research into these kinds of drawings and watercolours, and it was quite difficult, since apart from the well-known, mainly Dutch artists there was then very little documentation about the mass of lesser-known painters and botanists and their work.

I love the large amount of space we have in London, although I don't particularly need it all, but it is untypical in a city and it is rather like having a large bag and filling it when a smaller one would do. One of the joys here is that Patrick and I each have our own bathroom. Mine has been left more or less as it was before, in a light brown marble and pale blue paper, but the other one we have tiled like an old dairy. The cupboards, which were also here before we came, are well-designed and very roomy, so they are ideal for my working life as there is masses of space for hatboxes, shoes, gloves and formal clothes. I do try and organise myself a day in advance if I am working but this rarely happens, and I tend to end up sewing on a button in rather a panic. I organise my clothes myself, although it would be the greatest luxury to have a lady's maid. My mother had a maid for a short time, and from her I learnt several useful things which have stood me in good stead. For example, she taught me to pack properly, with lots of tissue paper, which I still do, although Patrick just throws everything into a bag. I keep all my clothes from years back, although most of the hats get re-cycled into the children's dressing-up box.

All the photographs and pictures in my bedroom are of immense importance to me. We have several pictures of the children, and one of the paintings near our bed, by Derek Hill, is of a ruined church on an island on Lough Erne in Northern Ireland where I grew up. When I look at the wild sky and the grey of the water in the picture, it immediately takes me back to childhood picnics and summer days spent there. I know that this island is where I would like to be buried.

As a child I also spent quite a lot of time in London in Bourdon House, Bond Street, which is now Malletts. It was a labyrinth of dark and narrow eighteenth-century passages which were curtained with red and white striped damask that waved in the draughts, and my bedroom there was a tall slit with a high window to the sky surrounded by rather depressing pea-green curtains and an old grey carpet. My parents appeared to believe more in the functional aspect of a child's room rather than the look, and our rooms in Ireland were also plain and practical. I had a wallpaper of grey and white spots with which I played many visual games, joining the spots up to make all sorts of shapes, and the cracks in the ceiling were as much fun. Later my mother let us choose what we wished for our rooms and tried to steer us gently away from the gaudy wallpapers that we thought looked so wonderful – but for years the bedroom always seemed more of a banishment place, either for bad behaviour or *having* to go to sleep. I think one should enjoy one's bedroom, because one spends so much time in it, and I have taken trouble with our children's bedrooms for that reason.

As we have a family life and business meetings here, there are times when I feel the need for absolute privacy. Paradoxically, I find it easier to get away from people here in London than in the country. My bedroom here feels private and secure, although the street is just outside, whereas at Shugborough the public is often just under the windows and I feel that I must be up and doing. But here, when I want to escape I can close the bedroom door, turn off the telephone, and lie on my bed to read or just to think. I get up early every morning to cook my husband's breakfast, so I can only lie in when Patrick is away. Occasionally, someone comes to give me a massage, and I love to lie flat on the floor to relax and recharge. Yet however private one's bedroom feels, it is still inescapably a part of everyday life: the alarm clock set for seven, the school report on the bedside table, the sight of a pair of shoes that needs to go to the menders. Thus I feel it is very important to make the time to get away together to an utterly different setting, even if only occasionally. Our bedroom in Mustique, where we can escape for holidays, is in complete contrast to this room. Instead of the softer, subtler feel we aimed for here, it is a bare cool room in pale shades of green with white, with a little locally carved double bed in bleached wood. From there one can return with a fresh perspective on one's surroundings and the fast-moving pace of everyday life.

A view into the bedroom from the hall, where a wallpaper border of sweetpeas runs around the door. Eighteenth-century wooden hall chairs stand beneath botanical prints.

The Countess of Lichfield at her dressing-table. On the wall above hang a portrait of herself by Molly Bishop and pictures of her children.

DIANA POTTER

Diana Potter, an executive producer at Thames Television, lives in an eighteenth-century Gothic gatehouse in the country and a flat in London. She was formerly a journalist.

There is a price to be paid for falling in love with a house, however rewarding the final result. In my own case it involved juggling with three abodes at once. Despite my determination not to, I succumbed to the lure of this aptly named folly in a Capability Brown park. It is tiny and idiotically grand, like a fantasy castle in a children's book. It stands halfway down an overgrown drive in the middle of the park, deserted and romantic. It had been empty for three years, and it showed. The arch, the tower and even the flint rustications were covered with nettles and elder, and weeds were sprouting everywhere. It was exceedingly dark, facing north-east, and the walls were running with damp, but I fell for it. Having done so, I had to exchange my house in London for a flat, and a comfortable, attractive and sunny London bedroom for one that faces due north and appears to have been designed for one purpose and one purpose only – financial reasons have, as yet, prevented me from removing the 'poule de luxe' look.

In the country a sunny bedroom was therefore especially important, but my bedroom at the Lodge did not augur well. It had only a single round *oeil-de-boeuf* window, facing north-east, and the steeply pitched roof made it impossible to stand upright in one third of the room. The whole place was running with damp, an ideal climate for the frogs that were rumoured to play around the house by night. I simply could not face this gloom and discomfort. By inserting two dormer windows into the pitched roof not only can I stand comfortably in the whole bedroom but

the south sun has now transformed the room. Because I had to wait for the damp of years to dry out I decided to paint all the walls of the room white, not wanting to waste money until I am certain that the last damp patches have disappeared.

The next problem was curtains. *Oeil-de-boeuf* windows are virtually impossible to curtain successfully – a straight curtain just looks pathetic marooned in the middle of a wall, and any attempt at frills and furbelows looks extremely pretentious. In the end, I was advised to leave the window plain. The solution was to have made a piece of blockboard with magnetic clips that slot exactly into the porthole shape, so that the glass can be screened when I want to sleep late and keep out the light, or when the weather is very cold. As it happens, I hardly use the device at all. The Gothic dormers presented another problem, but I had noticed the way a friend dealt with similar windows, and I copied her idea. Each curtain is attached to a brass rod which, when the curtain is opened, hinges back so that the curtain hangs against the reveal of the window.

My bedroom is very small. It just takes a tallboy, a bed, and a tiny dressing-table which is really just set-dressing, as I make up in the bathroom next door. The bed itself is a five-footer, and I find that I miss it dreadfully when I am put to stay somewhere in a single one, and I invariably roll out. The older generation tends to raise an eyebrow if you are single and have a large bed, rather in the same way that an aunt of mine will give you a gin that would put an elephant under the table, but grimace with disapproval if a woman asks for a whisky.

I have a habit of using my bed as a desk, with books, papers, recorder and telephone piled all around me on the covers, and I usually have three books on the go at once, depending on what mood I'm in: heavy, light or a detective novel. I don't have a television in my bedroom, because enough is enough.

On Sunday mornings I spend much of the time in bed with a number of newspapers and a copious amount of coffee. Newsprint does make the sheets filthy, but I am certainly not as well disciplined as a friend of mine who puts a towel over the bed before she starts reading. I had heard of the pre-War habit of ironing newspapers, but until I read Kenneth Clark's autobiography I had not realised that the purpose of ironing papers with blotting paper was to remove the excess ink.

It has only just dawned on me quite how rigid I am about bedrooms. I hate coloured or patterned sheets, and feel the same about coloured baths and lavatories. Duvets give me a vague sense of unease because they make the bed look lumpy, and I am never sure if they are really hygienic. I would give them to children, even so, because they are simpler than hospital corners, but never to grown-ups. At school we used to be made to strip our beds every morning and fold the sheets and blankets into a neat pile, and one friend who stays with me does it still. When I was poor I used to have the most amazing selection of army surplus blankets, and it was a real treat finally to be able to go and get some good ones – white, of course. And I do like pretty pillowcases. My sheets seem to have lasted rather well, and so I have not yet had to put the sides to middles, which is

Between the windows overlooking the garden is a dressing-table in fruitwood and a small eighteenth-century looking glass. The curtains show an ingenious solution to dressing windows in the Gothic shape: the blue and white Greek seersucker cotton is hung on hinged brass rods which open outwards, with the bottom of the curtains held by a clasp.

Diana Potter at one of her cottage windows.

what a lot of my well brought-up friends were taught to do.

My bed needs a bedhead, and I would like it to be the same Gothic shape as the windows, but this would not work because one never lies in the middle of the bed, and one's head would constantly be hitting the wall. When I was small, my idea of heaven was a four-poster, but now I have slept in several in friends' houses I have reservations. To start with, the swing of the curtain makes reading in bed almost impossible as the light is always too far back, and being a smoker, all the hangings of my four-poster would have to be cleaned every two months.

There are so many bedroom accoutrements that seem to have disappeared. An aunt once gave me a very pretty slip of material to lay over my smalls at night, and I still have friends who have chamber pots. I do have a hot-water bottle cover though, that my mother bought in Florence, which is a very chic number and replaces the old knicker-pink woollen one I was given as a child. The worst experience I ever had with a hot-water bottle was when staying with another aunt in the country. We had been to a party and I went to bed about four in the morning, feeling rather cold. Having put the bottle down between the sheets, I turned to undress and then thought the room must be on fire. I saw clouds of steam rising from the bedding. When I told an older friend years later about this, she looked at me with pity and replied, 'Did your mother never advise you to go to bed in a mackintosh, if you remotely suspected that your hostess had not aired your sheets?'

I have worked for over twenty years as a journalist and television producer, and this has entailed a great deal of travelling. 'You *are* lucky to travel so much' is the usual envying remark, but to be transplanted out of one's own bedroom into depersonalised international hotels is not always fun, and anyway one is usually working very hard. Because of the Union rules it is always civilised – a bathroom and a bedroom to oneself – but generally the room is too small, the bed not too comfortable and the decoration, except in a very few cases, appalling. And the rooms are always stiflingly hot. There is an enormous sense of relief in getting back to one's own bed and room after weeks of filming. It is the only place to be quiet in, or to be ill in, and I always feel a sense of pleasure when I walk into my own bedroom.

Diana Potter's simple country bedroom with a Laura Ashley bedside lamp below the circular oeil-de-boeuf *window; the bed is covered with a nineteenth-century cotton quilt patterned with red tulips and blue flowers on a cream background.*

TESSA KENNEDY

Tessa Kennedy is a partner in an international interior design company, which she founded sixteen years ago, and her designs for clients range from palaces to hospitals. Her house in the country near Windsor is Victorian. She has four sons and a daughter, aged from twenty-five to twelve.

I was fifteen before I had a bedroom of my own: until then I shared with my twin sister, Marina. The room of my own was lavishly decorated by my mother, who transformed it into a tent cocooned with what I am sure was a mile of *toile de jouy*, a fabric that was particularly favoured in the Fifties. I think my mother was heavily influenced in this choice by a film she admired called *Desirée*, a romantic celluloid version of Napoleon's liaison with one of his mistresses. I don't know whether any of this romanticism rubbed off on me, but it was from this room that, at the age of seventeen, I ran away to get married.

An earlier influence on my taste was undoubtedly my grandmother, Madame Banac, with whom we lived in America for five years during the war. She had her own very definite style of luxury and grandeur with a vast house on the Hudson River, which because of its location and atmosphere reminds me of the Victorian house that is now my home.

Because my house is forever filled with my children and their friends, I have always made my bedroom an off-limits sanctuary, the frontier post at which all others must halt. I suppose, in truth, I am basically a night person, so it was important to me to design my bedroom unlike any other room in the house. It is somewhere that I can isolate myself and resolve most of my problems, calmed by the early morning sun streaming in through my windows.

An ornate Victorian Gothic four-poster dominates the bedroom. The materials are a mix of cotton, lawn, linen, lace and broderie anglaise, and the paint colours in the room are cool and pale.

On the windowsill to the left of the bed stand cut-out photographs of Tessa Kennedy's three sons while schoolboys at Eton.

I sleep in a huge four-poster, one of those carved wood Strawberry Hill Gothic beds which sometimes make the occupants feel that they are not so much lying in bed as lying in state. When we first moved into the house, I spurned the existing Windsor-soup brown decor in the bedroom, although in some ways it was appropriate for a large, basically dark house. Instead, I opted for cool colours and tranquillity. I rag-rolled the walls in apple-green glaze, taking advantage of the fact that the room has windows on two sides overlooking and indeed overlooked by the garden. Since I always try to keep the bedroom filled with fresh flowers, the impression is that the garden and the room merge.

This large dark bed was a later addition, but to tie in with the overall pale theme I covered it with fine white cottons, lawns and lace. This combination of Gothic architecture and starched white lace distinctly

reminds me of being in church. All my bed linen and towels are white. I hate new sheets and towels, and am only happy when they are soft and well worn. For this reason, I love using antique lawns and linen, because the running-in has been done by someone else. I also have a passion for hand-made lace and I find the machine-made variety a very poor imitation. I am definitely not a spartan, if being spartan means that a person is content to sleep on a mattress on the floor. I love mattresses stuffed with sheep's wool, pure goose-down pillows, soft cashmere blankets in the winter and light, pure down eiderdowns in the summer.

A previous owner was a landscape gardener, and from my bed I look into the branches and over the tops of some rare and beautiful old trees, some dating back to the fifteenth century. There is an ancient cedar, and three cypresses which are the only ones remaining from an avenue. In summer there is a huge splatter of yellow from a group of laburnums. When I bought the place it was completely drowned in wisteria and ivy, much of which was pulled down by the builders, but they are beginning to grow back again. I have added climbing roses and honeysuckle which have just begun to peep round my window. The scent of honeysuckle in my bedroom instantly takes me back to my childhood, when every summer was spent at a place called Guerney's Inn at Montauk on the tip of Long Island in New York State. We stayed at an enchanted bungalow on the beach which was dripping in scented honeysuckle, a very evocative smell.

I have made my bedroom into an intensely personal retreat which I never tire of. I have collections of family photographs and mementos – pictures of the children at various ages by my bedside, books written by friends kept close at hand, paintings that hold particular pleasure for me and piles of magazines. The fireplace surround, the round table in the bay window and the large windowsill, my desk and my bedside tables are also cluttered with ornaments of all shapes and sizes, as well as more personal memorabilia. Ornaments appeal to me, and I have several different collections. One of these is a herd of assorted camels, made from every sort of material.

I have knocked two rooms into one to make a dressing room which connects with the bedroom and bathroom. All my clothes are kept in there, because I have an aversion to built-in wardrobes. I do have a magnificent Victorian clothes-stand on which I put out the clothes I am going to wear the following day.

Bathrooms should, in general, follow the colour scheme of the bedroom. This gives a more spacious feeling, even if the bathroom is tiny. Originally this house had fourteen bedrooms and two bathrooms, but it has now been converted to have seven of each. Just as I prefer white linen, I like white baths and basins; coloured bathroom suites are anathema to me. In my bathroom I have used a flowery American fabric for the curtains. The pretty colours of this material echo the garden theme that I have created in the bedroom. Having the bath in the middle of the room gives me yet another bird's eye view, this time of the croquet lawn. Behind my bath hangs a Pennsylvanian Dutch quilt, one of a collection of early

Tessa Kennedy framed in the front hall of her Victorian house.

A luxurious and restful new bathroom, with an antique quilt on the wall, leads off the bedroom.

American quilts that hang around the house.

Although there can be no set rules, I do believe that a bedroom should not just be a place where one spends a third of one's life, but should reflect a very personal taste and be an oasis of calm, a retreat, if you like, from the world beyond its walls. So many bedrooms are just treated as functional boxes, uninviting, featureless and impersonal. This I think is a pity, and I have tried to make my bedroom the one room to which I always long to return.

EMMA SERGEANT

Emma Sergeant is a successful portrait painter who graduated from the Slade in 1980. She lives alone in a London flat which she has adapted into an artist's studio. From her first floor balcony she looks into the tall trees of a square in South Kensington.

My ideal bedroom would be all glitter and gold leaf, like a lacquer box. The result of such extravagance would probably be in amazingly bad taste, and as I have no time to decorate my two bedrooms they stay as they are, stitched together with what I have. There is chintz raided from my mother, bric-à-brac from my old lady relations, and my collection of boxes. Oddly enough, whenever I'm given a present it is always some kind of a box. Perhaps people think I'm secretive.

I have very definite priorities. Painting is everything. If I go out it is to refresh myself, and I do not have any other interests; I don't really read unless I am on holiday when I wolf down books. My eyes are tired at the end of the day and I'm keen to start at the beginning of the day, so normally I have no time for anything else but my work.

My first place away from home with my parents in Highgate was with my cousin. I moved the first of my Milapote paintings there and lived with the smell of paint in his sitting room. I am extremely intolerant about living with other people, but as he had not decorated his flat and was away much of the time he was easy to live with. Making your place work really boils down to what you demand from it, and my flat is a private working space. Living with someone else depends on understanding the other person's working life and routine. If someone is taking care of you then you must have the time to take care of them, but I have indulged myself so much in my privacy that I do not have to face these problems.

Solitude is a most important thing to me, because if I see people I get rather tired. If I am going to see them at all, it has to be at certain times of day. I can stand on my feet to paint for twelve hours a day, but I cannot see people twelve hours a day. This means that my bedrooms are entirely for myself; because the two rooms are small, anyone else in them is rather like a bull in a china shop, and anyone coming to stay is one big fat intrusion. It is horrible.

When I was first looking for a studio flat I went to all the usual London places like Chelsea and Notting Hill Gate for a purpose-built artist's studio, but the prices were ridiculous. Then one day, driving through South Kensington, I saw this flat in an estate agent's window. I looked, and although it was at night and full of the mess from a family of four, I decided to take it. I loved the tall windows and the atmosphere, and I knew the square. It was not until later that I realised that the place faced north, with a beautiful cool light for painting. I built the minstrels' gallery, which is the bedroom I use for resting and where I sit to look down on my work, and there is a poky room at the back, with a token roof garden through the French windows, where I actually sleep. I retreat to these rooms but I do not spend much time in either place, or basking outside. Sometimes I go for a snooze in the bedroom, but more often I curl up on the bench by the radiator which is covered in my Aunty Rosy's ancient rug and blank out for twenty minutes. I have no problem relaxing, because if you physically tire yourself with work as I do, it is easy just to sit down and drop off to sleep. It is different if you work at a desk all day – then you simply feel mentally tired but physically tense. I have an immunity to anxiety, which means that I always sleep well.

When I am alone I play a lot of music: opera, and, because it flutters about drawing you into the passion then suddenly becoming light again, I listen to Mozart. I hate Bach; it is like a hypnotic rhythm going on next to your temple. And I adore the Rolling Stones, but at different times of day according to when I want music to pep me up. I am moody. Sometimes I wake feeling like a Vitamin A, B and C Girl, but at other times I need to lose myself completely in work. My mind goes off into extraordinary places when I'm painting, concentration flickering on and off, jumping into a strange wonderland.

The staircase leading to the bedroom upstairs appears in my paintings, because I like its shape, and so do other things of mine like my favourite blue and white cup and saucer and the apricot rug which I bought on holiday. I often paint my witch's ball, again because the shape interests me, but the result always looks surreal and ghastly.

I am practical, but I have very grand ideas about how I would like to do a place. I would like vast rooms. I do not like dottled, dibbled, scrottled effects of paint because I love plain white walls, and I cannot stand interiors with pale colours. I don't go for the boudoir effect, or all the incidental frou-frou of decoration in a bedroom. I would love to live in the heat, although it would be bad for my work, and I like the idea of a Spanish hacienda house with lovely dark red floor tiles, dark old wood, rugs, deep rich colours, arches and a porch. All that hot climate stuff. The alternative bedroom to the gold box, in my imagination of course, is a place where there is a low hard bed, tall dark wooden cupboards and shutters at the windows which open to overlook water nearby. If I were to start again with my flat I would get a new bed, have a high-pressure shower and tiles instead of the cork I put down, and hundreds more cushions upstairs. And copper – I am copper mad.

I am a deep red and a green person. All very unhealthy, since green is meant to be death and evil, but a lot of it creeps off my palette onto my work. I love high cool walls with rich red patterns against them. Blue is a natural colour that you take for granted, but I hate blue paint on walls and would never have a blue and white bedroom. Very unwelcoming and unsexy. I wear a lot of green, too. My cupboard space is pathetic and as I am untidy the clothes pile up in there. I tend to wear what is on top of the pile, linking it to what is next, and so work my way down to the floor. I love pretty clothes and a friend helps me choose them, but they all get lost in the cupboard. Just as I know that I can arrange flowers, so a friend knows about clothes and advises me on mine, and other people know about doing up their houses. It is a talent for a different kind of display. But I have no idea about which is the best lamp for a room, say, because I have never turned my mind and my eye to the matter. I do like a generous display though, a cornucopia, and whereas this is fine for a dressing-table and rather disastrous for clothes, it is rather a happy way to live. I hate stinginess.

There are a few things that I do mind about in the bedroom, and one of them is dirt. If I do not get around to cleaning and polishing it just pecks at my conscience, but real dirt troubles me. Getting into bed and finding grit on the sheets, dust blowing in from the balcony, all that.

I am very ambitious, and so one day when I am hugely successful and make a lot of money perhaps I will have the large bedroom I dream of and be able to employ people to look after everything. At the moment I see any form of decoration or buying furniture as an enormous treat only to be had when one has earned enough to set about getting it.

Meanwhile, I feel that I have come through four years of hard work and I need a breathing space. I feel I have earned my BA now, rather than when I officially graduated from the Slade, so now is the time when I can mentally spring clean. I have all these white walls and all the liberty which I hope I will soon be able to afford. So now my ideas are all going into a sort of mental filing cabinet, and my surroundings are a great melting pot for the ideas that fill my mind.

A collection of bric-à-brac and silk scarves in the small back bedroom.

Emma Sergeant sitting beneath a panel of one of her prize-winning pictures.

MARY VANGO

Mary Vango is a freelance make-up artist. Earlier in her career she worked for several years as a photographic and fashion model. She lives in a flat in a 1930s apartment block in Willesden, in north-west London.

The furniture and fittings throughout my bedroom, bathroom and dressing room area, like those in most of the flat, came from the demolished wing of the Savoy Hotel, and I was lucky enough to acquire everything through a friend of mine who deals in Art Deco.

Looking back on all my past bedrooms, it would be true to say that they have all had a common aim, which was to create a somewhat unreal, fantasy surrounding. For me, living within the realms of practicality hinders my own creativity, leaving nothing for the imagination to feed on.

It seems almost a cliché to say that a person's life is reflected in the environment in which they live. We can never exist without some sort of environment, as that is the basis of our everyday lives. Yet I believe that within our reality there is another dimension – one that has nothing to do with the physical aspect of life. Therefore, I create environments for my inner life, ones that are conducive to allowing thoughts to take form, and in so doing adopt a more concrete aspect. I produce a setting that allows my thought processes to formulate without the distraction of the outside world. If you allow your imagination to take over, there are infinite directions in which it can go.

On the practical side, however, achieving this involves a lot of expense and energy, as well as headaches, because it is sometimes difficult to convey rather abstract ideas to the people who will implement them. They get things wrong, so you have to take the time to rethink and find a way to improvise with the result. I am an appalling perfectionist. This bed was

In the bedroom suite original fitments from the Savoy Hotel in London mix with a tulle canopy over the bed: an unusual hybrid resulting from a love of Jazz Age chic and the languor of mosquito-netted rooms in the stories of Somerset Maugham. The doorway leads to the entrance hall of the flat, and a zebra-skin rug lies on the fitted carpet.

made three times, and although they were given specific measurements the shape of the bedhead, which incorporates a radio, music and headphones, is still not exactly right.

The principal but not so obvious theme within this area is Oriental, with the addition of Western necessities like telephones, effective lighting and music. The blossom tree and the mosquito net are reminiscent of my early days. I grew up in Australia and also, for part of my childhood, lived in Singapore, where mosquito nets were of the utmost importance if one was to get a peaceful night's sleep. Inspiration is also drawn from anything around me, a film or a ballet that I have seen, maybe a book that I have read. Even driving down a road can instil in my head a certain image which I will later incorporate into the design in some way. I am always adding and subtracting; I never maintain a constant, rigid positioning of ornaments and furniture. My thoughts will travel in one direction, but before I know it, I am thinking of another theme – all of which does not mean I am susceptible, but that I am eager to experiment and learn. My whole flat has a framework, and within these boundaries I have allowed myself the freedom to explore and develop.

My main source of inspiration stemmed from old Hollywood movies with their 1930s brilliance and splendour, especially some of Eric von Stroheim's work. Another strong contemporary influence is the sophistication of Fellini's films, with *Juliet of the Spirits* and *Satyricon* immediately springing to mind. These images are at once sexual and provocative. My last bedroom was a dark den with an olive-green satin tent and the bed on a raised platform, obviously quite different from the present one. When I bought this flat there was something going on in my life that made me want to wake up to a softer, light room – one that had sunlight streaming in, with lots of windows and open spaces. My next bedroom, I think, will be Japanese in style, with the feeling of living on an island.

The predominant colour here is pink, with splashes of cream; mirrors and chrome decorate most of the surfaces, and the only two pictures I have on the walls are by the English artist Charles Wheeler. They are sensual, serene and feminine, which are the main elements of the overall atmosphere, emphasised by the zebra skin on the floor.

Lighting is another element of vital importance to me. The results achieved with effective lighting can be astounding, even in an empty room. The first objective here was to eliminate central overhead light, so allowing one to create shadows, which are most interesting and pleasing to the eye. Three small spots illuminate the folds in the pink curtains, whilst also lighting the blossom tree, constructed from dead branches and tiny silk flowers, which is an essential part of the Oriental illusion.

There are no doors throughout the bedroom, dressing room and bathroom areas; firstly, because I loathe them, and secondly because they are cumbersome. Without doors one can create a feeling of open space with no restrictions, and by lining the dressing-room walls with floor-to-ceiling mirrored wardrobes, another mysterious dimension is created, recalling Orson Welles' *Hall of Mirrors*. Above the dressing-room doorway I have put a 'Ladies' Room' sign, to create an illusion of privacy within an open space.

When friends come into the flat they do, on the whole, seem to adapt to my way of thinking. I feel that if one designs with too much practicality in mind, one loses the flow and lives within the restrictions of normality. If I decide the net over the bed needs to be elsewhere I will reposition it, although that probably means a mad night when I choose to act on my whim at some ungodly hour. The mosquito net was erected, after many hours of deliberation, in a burst of activity shortly before dawn that almost caused me to break a leg. I piled chairs on top of the bed to reach the ceiling, rather than find the step-ladder, and of course I toppled down to the floor swamped in tulle.

I am incredibly tidy – to the point of obsessiveness – and I know precisely where everything is.

As a make-up artist I am employed every day to put make-up on models, producing images for certain products, and in a job like this you have to be extremely efficient. If I need three tubes of a foundation cream, I know just where to find them. Everything has to have its right place, because as I work such funny hours I do not want to come home to meet disorganisation.

Winter clothes are in one wardrobe, summer clothes in another and shirts in yet another; hats in hat boxes, jewellery in glass jars on the bathroom unit, scarves on the inside of the wardrobe doors and shoes on the bottom. The aim is to eliminate all the fluster, so allowing an atmosphere of quiet luxury.

When I have lived with someone on a long-term basis, it seems that my personality overpowers his need to be untidy, and he ends up appreciating the order. I would not accept it otherwise. I could not possibly go around picking up clothes for someone. It is totally unnecessary. People must always respect their partner's personality and never subject them to mess. If you persevere, eventually men do get the point. Most people can live with a normal degree of chaos, but I feel if I were a man it would be quite refreshing to come into a place which was immaculate and aesthetically pleasing – but maybe this is just my personality. I do get the feeling that the flat is sometimes too imposing, making too strong a statement, to put it mildly, but in the end people realise that this is me. I am very feminine and I have strong opinions, which I need to voice at all times.

My bedroom inspires me and helps to make the outside world bearable. It coaxes the mind from madness back to tranquillity, and refreshes the sleepy body in times of need, because those repetitive grey English dawns can reduce even the most active to a state of lethargy. The ambiance of the bedroom is continued throughout the dressing room and bathroom, making an entity to render one oblivious to the harsh reality outside. The whole little complex is my sanctuary, especially whilst getting ready to go out. There are speakers throughout the area, and a telephone in easy reach of the bath while I lie in it, with a glass of champagne to quench the thirst, slowly letting my body and mind unwind and thinking of much more important things, such as what to wear.

Mary Vango, wearing a sequinned Thirties' dress, in her dark, glittery dining room.

Blackamoor heads on pedestals stand either side of the entrance to the dressing room and bathroom. One turban holds fake branches of almond blossom. A sign marked 'Ladies Room' hangs over the mirror-framed entrance.

Sundays are my favourite days and are spent for the most part in bed, either watching television, making telephone calls or reading the newspapers. Unless there is a lunch party to go to the day is literally spent within the confines of this room. There are many facets of the original concept which are still unexplored, so the bedroom will always be in a constant state of transition, reflecting the elements of my character.

Pink and black marble, bottles of Chanel, sleek fittings and Palm Court greenery: all recapture an era. The reflection in the mirror over the hand-basin shows shelves full of Twenties' and Thirties' bric-à-brac.

DR CHRISTIAN CARRITT

Dr Christian Carritt is a London doctor and a graduate of Somerville College, Oxford. She lives with her young son and his nanny in a South Kensington flat, from where she runs her practice. For reasons of limited space, the doctor's surgery is also the mother's bedroom.

I love this room: it is my world. I've always enjoyed bed-sitting room life; I loved it at Oxford, and I would be very happy ending up in a bed-sitting room with everything at arm's length. I like hibernating with cosiness around me, and I really don't long to walk down corridors or climb upstairs to my bed.

I moved into the room in 1981, when I came back from abroad. Before I went away I had had two connected flats for my home and my practice, but on my return one flat had to house my work, myself, and my son and his nanny. So, to start my practice again, I gave my bedroom to the nanny and the little boy, and I decided to make a surgery-bedroom in the old dining room. From then the room evolved round me. My bed also became the examination couch, and I had to share the only bathroom with the patients. As I spend most of the day in my bedroom I decided to put all my favourite pieces of furniture in this room, because I love them, and I wanted my patients to enjoy them too.

I have collected and inherited a lot of family furniture and I am very attached to family possessions. The room has slowly got fuller and fuller, and I change everything around from time to time. I am surrounded by indoor plants, as a substitute for a garden. My plants are not very beautiful and a lot of them are cast-offs, but I like to watch them grow and come back to life. I move them about a great deal, and they all get turns on the windowsill. I get pleasure from the grouping of my clutter, and

The doctor's surgery-bedroom has an atmosphere that is warm but efficient. The desk and the Victorian oak chairs with their original plush seats were inherited from the owner's twin brother.

although I don't always do the grouping well I like to alter things and give familiar ornaments a fresh perspective.

I don't like the clinical appearance of most doctors' surgeries. I dislike pretentiousness. I am old-fashioned and have not moved with the times, and so I have no beautiful, modern, well-designed vilene trays, and so on. Instead, I have old ones that I have found around the house, and I use an old tin hat box with a lid as a wastepaper basket, because I cannot bear the appearance of rubbish in an open basket. Now that I have a surgery-bedroom I never want my surgery to look clinical again. We are moving to a house soon, and I do not mind if my kitchen there looks functional, but I don't want my surgery to look like a hospital room even though it will run efficiently. Behind the cupboard doors there will be lots of brightly coloured containers for specimen jars, syringes, needles and other necessities, but I shall put pretty pleated silk behind the glass doors of the cupboards to disguise the *batterie de medicine*. The metal filing cabinet, an eyesore which I cannot dispense with, will live in another room, and I am going to transform my examination couch into a deliciously inviting chaise longue, fit for an odalisque, covered with old paisley shawls.

I like the patients to feel at home and I like Victoriana, and as my practice is rather an eccentric one and I'm rather an eccentric person, I want my consulting room to have an individual style of its own. It reflects me. The patients who like me will like this surgery, and if they don't, they will go elsewhere. My room reflects my personality, which I'd like to think is efficient but relaxed and easy-going. I do not want to give the impression of being a remote and unapproachable doctor.

My room is the only room in the flat where I have hung the pictures properly. Some of them were inherited from patients, but the majority were left to me by my twin brother David, whom I adored. I find these possessions very sad and very comforting at the same time. The picture of the girl in the snow is by Townley Greene, and I think it must have been an illustration for a book, although I don't know which book. My other pictures are all Victorian, and most of them are in their original frames. As I am not a grand person and I like quiet domesticity, I find all my pictures very *gemütlich*. At the end of the day, when I have finished with the patients, I like to look at my pictures in their maple-wood frames, especially the picture of sheep grazing in the English countryside at harvest time, which came from David's cottage in Farringdon.

I also have my brother's collection of fairground lustre, his bamboo furniture and his shell boxes. I sit at his desk, which is too small for my work, simply because I love it, and I am also extremely fond of the saddleback chairs with their original green plush covers. Our styles in decoration are quite similar, but he possessed more things, particularly as I spent ten years abroad and had to give many of my possessions away. I have my own collection of pin cushions, mostly made by sailors in the nineteenth century, which was augmented by my brother's collection. I am not mad about everything in my room, but some of the objects I love purely because of their associations and I intend to keep them.

Years ago the walls in my room were covered in blue bookbinding material with linen curtains dyed to match, but while I was abroad my tenant painted everything Dior grey. When I came to re-decorate the room I ordered some wallpaper from a decorating shop, but sadly the paper did not materialise in time, so I chose the present nondescript greeny-grey paint from a colour chart in ten minutes. It is inoffensive and restful, and a good background to Victorian paintings in general and maple-wood frames in particular.

Originally I had a huge brass central hanging lamp with a green shade, which must once have hung over a billiard table, but when the room changed from being a dining room to become my bedroom it was unsuitable. At present I have an Empire glass hanging lamp which is particularly out of keeping with the rest of the room, but nobody notices, and it is serviceable and very pretty.

I have to keep everything as tidy as I can. I do get in a muddle, and my muddle is visible. I don't like to hide everything in drawers and cupboards, so at the weekends I reorganise myself. I catch up with the paperwork, do the filing, and by Monday morning it is clean and neat and tidy for the patients and the secretaries.

My room at Somerville College, Oxford, was the first room of my own. Before that, during the War, and again later, I always had to share my room. I shared with my sister in the family home in Holland Villas Road; then, when she and my brother were given rooms of their own, I had to share mine with a cousin in the WAAF, who was posted to London during the War. To have a bed-sitting room of my own at Oxford was paradise, and from that moment on I think my world has always revolved around my bedroom. My bedroom became the room where I could have my own life – but perhaps everybody thinks this about their bedroom.

My bedroom is the only room I have that is private, and I still consider it

Dr Carritt seated below a picture of a young woman in the snow by Townley Greene. On the left is part of her collection of fair-ground lustre.

private even when I am seeing my patients there. Nobody will ever walk into this room without being asked to do so. Luke, my son, never comes in without first knocking on the door, and even then he expects me to go to the door to find out what he wants. At night it is different. He likes to tuck me up in bed and make sure I have my book; he kisses me goodnight, and then he departs. I am in my little world, content and happy, and I am the world's best sleeper.

A Victorian oil painting of people fishing off rocks and the collection of objects below it, including nineteenth-century pincushions, reflect Christian Carritt's love of Victoriana.

ANITA RODDICK

Anita Roddick is managing director of The Body Shop International, a multi-million pound cosmetic company which she founded in 1976. Mrs Roddick's previous careers include teaching English and History at a Comprehensive school and running a hotel and restaurant with her husband, Gordon. The Roddicks live with their two teenage daughters, Justine and Samantha, in a seventeenth-century flintstone farmhouse on the edge of the Sussex downs.

In our bedroom we set out to achieve total anonymity. Now, when I am told it looks and feels like a suite in a well-appointed hotel, this is the highest compliment that could be paid. Our objective was a matter-of-fact space simply for sleep, that is all. If we are not asleep in the room then we are hardly in it. I have no feelings about the room, and now that we are down to the final details of its organisation, I am neither pleased nor displeased with the results, and my detachment is success in itself. Basically, this bedroom is another item on our agenda.

The room is a stopover between one busy day and the next, and when we are not away travelling round the stores or abroad, we leave the house each morning by seven and rarely return before eight at night, unless I am at home for our girls' school holidays. There is little of real value in here, or indeed in the house, because the real financial investment which gives us pleasure to look at has gone into the walls with the techniques of stippled paintwork and airbrushing. However, I might add that my daughter is already fed up with the airbrushed geese and flamingos on her bedroom furniture.

When we bought this house, it had been left untouched for forty years and everything was in a state of near decay. It was also the sum total of

A business-like bedroom, with bedhead and curtains in thick grey silk piped in red and a bold blue and red bedspread, reflected in the arched and mirrored doors of wall-to-wall cupboards. To the left, the door slides to screen the entrance to the bathrom, and the dressing room passage is to the right.

every design mistake that I had made myself in the last twenty years, so I was given the opportunity to start again from scratch.

We were able, because of the success of our business, to have a place just the way I want it to be. Plans were discussed immediately, but the action delayed, because one of the best tricks when doing up a house is to let the place remain as you find it for six months. The classic mistake which anyone can make is sweeping change on arrival, and the wisdom in biding your time is that after a few months of living in a place, you know what you want to do with it. For example, the most interesting architectural feature in our house is the arched window between the two half-landings on the staircase leading to our bedroom. When I came to re-vamp the bedroom, I realised how much satisfaction there was in the rise of this arch, so the frame became the inspiration for the design of the fitted cupboards. Later, I filled the arches with mirror to accentuate their shape and introduce more light, and the result is more interesting than a wall of plain dark wood.

The one exception to our delaying tactics was the kids' rooms, which we fixed up on moving in, so that each of them had her own oasis of sanity, complete with a carpet. We slept on a mattress on bare boards.

After considering all the options for the room, I knew that it was to be a masculine bedroom. This decision was for three reasons. First, the room had to appeal equally to both my husband and myself, since it is shared. Secondly, it had to be efficient because of our demanding professional life, and last and perhaps the strongest reason of all three was that I realised I have a natural and absolute phobia about feminine, frilly bedrooms.

The next step was how to put the idea into practice. The element of masculinity could be conveyed both by colour and by a lack of eclectic pretty objects. The decision about colour was quite difficult because if you are a victim of fashion, as I am, then you recall the now dated purples and beige of the Sixties, the pastels and whatever else of the Seventies, and I knew that if the room was to have a lifespan of about ten years before re-decoration it must look timeless. A good safe background colour was required which I could use to play around with tones and texture, so I decided on grey as the base. Next, we had to cope with the shape of the room, because the foundations had fallen slightly, leaving the walls and floor askew, and the rebuilding of this led me to the design of the cupboards and ultimately the positioning of the bed. Having settled on the colour and the structural alterations, which included the addition of a window seat, the rest was trial and error. From here on, all you have to do if you want to get a room done up quickly is to be a good plagiarist. Loads of magazines were brought in to study, and I made trips to every design exhibition on in London; within a week I had resolved the next part of the programme, but not, I might add, without my share of mistakes.

This is not designed to be a sybaritic room where you can flounce around and pamper yourself, because I do not spend time in the narcissistic habit of scrubbing and embalming myself. We have surfaces that are as convenient as those in a workroom instead of a dressing-table, and the clothes are out of the way. It is important to me that clothes

Businesswoman Anita Roddick relaxes in jeans on her bedroom window seat looking out on the garden.

should be hidden, and this is probably a hangover from my early days, when my parents had to hang all our clothes on a rail. I know that even our open passage dressing room is a mistake, because it has to be kept tidy, so I am about to cover that up. The time factor is vital in my life so I have to be self-disciplined, whereas given half a chance my nature is to drop clothes all over the place. We try to curtail this by having an efficient niche for everything. In our business there is no time to be wasted hunting for clothes, and I cannot ever allow myself to engage in the universal worry of, 'Oh my God, what am I going to wear today?'

Having found our pewter-coloured wallpaper and the drapes with their edges piped in crimson, for all of which I enlisted the advice of a decorating shop rather than risk hours of experimentation, I then made an error. It was a crucial one. I mean the bedcover, which I think is hideous, though at least ninety percent of other people like it. It is much too heavy and it does not fit over the bed properly, since I managed to muddle the specifications for the bed frame and the cover. The bedside lamps could be better for reading by and their shape improved upon, and they will be replaced when one day I apply myself to the task. Gordon and I have different patterns of sleep, so the ideal lamps would be discreet spotlights we can read by without disturbing each other, but such lighting tends to be ugly. Also, we paid attention to our builder rather than heeding our own instincts, and have landed up with too few recessed ceiling lights. All these imperfections come down to my lack of expertise in the field and the tremendous pressures on our time.

Although a hotel bedroom is close to my ideal, there is nothing worse than having a bathroom at home that is too clinical. The room could have been very cold, and I was aware that every surface that was patterned or graphic would date, so I concentrated on the architraves as these are timeless. The bath was found in France and shipped over, and then, just for a touch of pizazz and fun, I installed the star-dressing-room bulbs and mirror over the washbasins. Now I can test the products we make in a functional space, and because the bathroom is tiled it can be wiped clean in five minutes.

Along the corridor we have a different and totally outrageous little bathroom where the hand-basin is shaped like a luscious lady's backside and the shelf above it resembles her buxom bosom. When the unsuspecting visitor walks in there is usually a pause, followed by howls of laughter. It is simply a surprise, and opening a door to find a surprise, like the children's story of *The Secret Garden*, is the kind of thing I like. Both the china lady and the bare bulb mirror notions are my bit of kitsch, a harmless dash of Golders Green.

For many women there is a physical joy in dressing and choosing clothes for themselves, and although I love textures, I have a terrible, dumb guilt about spending money on myself. I can only put this down to a Catholic upbringing, where selflessness meant not wasting time in the bathroom or on yourself and, as it happens, I do believe that life is much more exciting than looking at yourself in the mirror.

As this bedroom is intended to be anonymous, pragmatic and timeless, it is not a setting for intimacy. I think that if you have been married, and happily so, for fifteen years, and you have a terrific working relationship going as well, you do not feel it necessary to have a room where romance is brought up to date. That would be the stuff of fantasy. After fifteen years you have progressed onto a different plane of great friendship and love, and falling in lust is unlikely; nor is the setting of your room going to evoke an arena for fresh flesh. If I were single, divorced, or a widow then I might have a different outlook, and if you are immersed in a great love affair then you will probably conduct it all over the place, the bedroom being the last place you get around to.

We did have notions about breakfast in bed, but once you cart the stuff upstairs it is either cold or has dropped on the floor. Swanning about with trays is great for B-movies, but in the reality of family life you go and eat downstairs with the kids.

The work ethos has played a very large part in the decisions I have made about the house and in the way I run it, and is inherent in the way the bedroom is done up. My mother became the family provider when she was widowed, and from the age of nine I helped her in the restaurant she was left to run on her own. We were an unconventional family; we might well be described as the original latchkey kids. I grew up sharing a room with my sisters, and even now I am devoid of any need for privacy or space to myself. This probably accounts for the fact that we are a very unprivate family ourselves, and the girls have always been free to come into our bed or to invade the bathroom.

I do not know a single working woman who has a hobby because she does not have the time for one, and yet there are plenty of professional women like myself who find housework positively therapeutic. For instance, last thing at night I will look around and view chaos: then half an hour later all is in order again, and by galloping about doing menial work I have become restored.

When I was on a visit to America in 1965, I realised what an enormous choice there was in packaging and in cosmetics, and what a good idea it would be to produce a range of products that would cleanse and polish

Teenage daughter Justine's bed-room, next door to her parents', has decorations in pale mauve with a design of bullrushes and geese; one of the specialist paint finishes in the house airbrushed by Alistair Macdonald.

the body, packaged in cheaper, simple containers like urine sample bottles. I was certain that there was a market for other women like myself who had to spin out a meagre sum of money and who needed one basic, affordable cream for the skin. So, after the ten-year gestation period of the idea, we launched our business in 1976 and have progressed from there.

Something must have happened in my early days to make me take nothing for granted, for possessions mean little to me, and my kick comes instead from my garden, in looking at flowers, and in the painfully slow but beautiful workmanship we have commissioned for the specialist wall finishes there. The accumulation of material things has never been of great significance to me, because everything in life is subject to change. I really do not believe that I am alive until I have woken up next morning, so every day to me is a bonus.

==

LADY SARAH ASPINALL

==

Lady Sarah Aspinall runs a flower shop, Curzon Lawrence Flowers, in Motcomb Street, London. She is married to John Aspinall, a gambler and zookeeper. They live in an eighteenth-century house in London's Belgravia and at Howletts Zoo Park in the country. Lady Sarah has three sons.

==

I call my bedroom my little area; it is the one place where I can be alone. Aspers has his vision of how the rest of the house should be, but in here I am allowed just to be myself. Every surface is cluttered and untidy, but it is arranged according to my nature. All my life is wrapped up in this room.

However, at the moment I'm *not* alone in here. Aspers recently announced that two of our new tigers would live with us during the week in London; as they are hand-reared, these little clubs are based with me.

Relaxation is desperately important, and I find that I can unwind best late at night when it is quiet, although I do snooze in the afternoons if I have been kept up by the cubs. At Howletts, they sleep in the bedroom until they are four months old, before progressing to the park, but this room becomes too restrictive after a couple of months. At the moment the dining room houses their play-pen, but soon we will have to find a larger enclosure. Tiger cubs love water, and they are apt to pounce into the bath, and on the arrival of someone unfamiliar to them they will dive under the bedcovers. When the tigers want to go to the lavatory they use a towel on the bedroom floor or go in a flower box, and we use miles of kitchen roll or the tissue paper from my dress boxes; proper house-training is an inappropriate discipline to impose on such animals.

Hand-rearing tigers is a tiring but rewarding business, and now, when I come into the room, they make a special whooshing sound of welcome which the Germans call *prusting*. The staff here take animals very much in

A tulip patterned glazed chintz from Osborne & Little is used for the bed, partnered by pale apricot satin cotton for the coronal and valance. The portraits on either side of the bed are of Jason and Amos Courage, two of Lady Sarah's sons.

their stride, and they remained quite calm when we had young wolves trotting about, and the baby gorilla to stay. The gorilla was particularly inquisitive; it would study its reflection in the mirrors, and like a small child was fond of fiddling with the objects on my dressing-table.

Aspers bought this house over twenty years ago and after our marriage, about six years later, we left the place much as it was. The coronal on the wall over the bed was already there, so eventually I changed the materials and the whole effect now reminds me of a glamorous Hollywood film set.

I appreciate a style where everything is in good order, but not to the extent that warmth and friendliness is lost. I am too lazy to run around looking for things, but luckily all the fabrics in here came from the shop of my brothers-in-law, Osborne and Little. I settled for this particular print because I love parrot tulips, and I find the material much more interesting than the usual rose chintz. All my favourite colours are in the stripes of the flowers. Coral is warm, welcoming, and shows off the furniture well. The yellow tapestry carpet was a present from my late husband, Piers, and if you half-close your eyes the shades all merge happily.

Aspers bought me the dressing-table. I like Biedermeier furniture, and I had seen that particular piece of furniture and longed for it. One day it was brought home to me as a present. The Biedermeier architect's desk came later, and I gradually added some chairs, but we are full up in here now and so I have to resist collecting further. The latest acquisition, a pretty writing desk, now lives in another bedroom.

I believe that a bedroom should always be romantic and interesting. Aspers prefers discreet lighting, particularly as he is asleep during the day, so when I want to do my make-up I scoot to the bathroom and pray that he will not emerge from his dressing room and switch off the light. We have dinner together in the evenings, usually at home or at his club with friends. When he gets back from work, I am leaving for Covent Garden to get flowers for my florist's business; we have been known to wave 'good morning' to each other in the dawn as we pass on the steps.

My correspondence lives in wicker baskets in my bedroom, and when one container overflows I move on to another, which is all part of my attempt to produce order from chaos, although poor Manuela and Helena would not agree. My cook and my lady's maid have been with me for many years now, and with Mrs Thorn, who has looked after us since my first son was born, they form a marvellous team. Manuela looks after my clothes, which are mostly kept in London; I only keep casual wear at Howletts and take everything else down when I need it. I seldom throw anything away, and there are clothes dating back as far as mini-dresses buried here, although I will never wear them again. I wear rather slim-fitting clothes and only have about four large ball dresses, so I do not need special storage space, but I have always admired those American ladies who have themselves perfectly organised with walk-in cupboards.

My treasure table lives in here, and there are certain places where my boys know I keep sweets. I like to think that all the objects in my room are approachable: my father's room always had lots of knick-knacks and games, and to me as a child it was an endless delight. We were allowed to play with everything. My sons are always delving into my cupboards, even if it is simply to spirit away my cashmere sweaters. The only thing I do not have among all these possessions is a television. But because I am so deaf, I use my bedroom in the same way as I do the car – somewhere I can turn the music up really loud. I play classical music such as Mahler and Sibelius, Oscar Petersen jazz and music from shows.

I do not make a special distinction between the styles of a bedroom in a town house and in a country house, although our room at Howletts happens to be larger and less flowery. This year the Howletts master bedroom will be re-designed by David Mlinaric, who has wonderful ideas as well as carte blanche in terms of costs from Aspers. David has a certain understanding of sumptuousness in decoration which I particularly admire, and Aspers is very good on detail, so together they did a marvellous job with the Aspinall Curzon, my husband's club, which I would describe as ostentatiousness just before it becomes bad taste. It seems perfect for that particular setting.

When I grew up we had a house in the country and I shared Nanny's bedroom there, until I was ejected into my own room, which was charming but rather frightening. I disliked the new room because I was convinced that there were ghosts around, and subsequently spent almost the entire time *under* the bed. During the week we had a house in Curzon Street, and I lived with Nanny in the nursery wing until I was older. But because things are seldom left to the daughters, I have very few objects from Penn, our family home, in my bedroom now. When I was in my late teens, I bought my own studio flat in South Kensington, and this is where Piers and I started our married life. The flat was cosy and warm, and in those days one just slung down a carpet and put up some chintz curtains. From there we moved to a house in Pimlico and had a lovely time decorating the bedrooms, although we had to change ours several times, and finished up sleeping in the dining room, as our three babies appeared like rabbits. Then we moved to a bigger house, but Piers was killed in a motor-racing accident, so he never saw the bedroom I made there.

I have a sentimental nature and tend to keep everything, especially anything given to me by the children. I cannot bear to throw anything away because everything has a special meaning, was presented at a particular moment, or reminds me of the babies, or whatever. I am nostalgic for the past – and even for the present – because, good or bad, each day has some little thing I want to remember it by.

If I daydream about other houses, I drift off into fantasies about those Gatsby-type mansions in America, which must have had wonderfully glamorous bedrooms. In my mind they are airy, elegant, full of laughter and happiness. The most memorable bedroom I have stayed in is at Le Haar, a Gothic castle in Holland built by the Van Zuylens towards the end of the last century, and still occupied by their descendants. Every bedroom was different, and each the size of a house, with incredible *objets* and beautiful furniture. At home I never loaf about eating breakfast in bed, looking glamorous and reading the newspapers, but the lifestyle there encouraged one to do just that. Anything in the world you wanted

Lady Sarah Aspinall with her two tiger cubs, named Bimha and Jumna after Indian rivers.

was brought on the most beautifully arranged tray, and the brioches and croissants were the tiniest, most delicate I have ever seen.

Aspers is incredibly generous and I would say that I have been a very spoilt woman, because I can run a lovely house and I am looked after in every possible way. A few years ago I became a freelance florist, and I have now opened a shop with my partner Lynne and several assistants. The business involves early morning telephone conversations with Lynne when we discuss the commissions for the day, which might be as many as a dozen different jobs for private parties and balls. Some of the best hours of the day are these, when I am down from my bedroom by five in the morning, earlier than anyone else. This is the time just for me and my work, when I wander about with my mug of coffee, place my flower orders, get up to date on plans for the garden, and have a quiet think.

A Japanese painting hangs over a Biedermeier architect's plans chest upon which are grouped a host of family photographs.

NINA CAMPBELL

Nina Campbell lives with her husband and three children in a mansion flat in Kensington. She is a designer, the head of an international decorating business.

I grew up in London and the first house that I remember was in Lowndes Square. It was so enormous that each floor was like a separate flat. Nanny and I had the third floor, and the rooms were vast and not particularly pretty. My parents had moved in just after the war, a time when I suppose everything was very difficult to get hold of. We moved like yo-yos when I was a child – round and round Belgravia. My father was a friend of the old Duke of Westminster, and the Grosvenor Estate was always very helpful in finding us houses. We lived in South Eaton Place, Lowndes Square, Chester Street, Chapel Street, Wilton Place and eventually Chester Square. Much later, I once suggested to my mother that she might move to Chelsea, but she replied, 'Darling, I have been a refugee from Vienna – why should I also be a refugee from Belgravia?'

I adored moving, as a child, because it always meant that I could choose a new bedroom. I can still remember all the various rooms, and I have been through most colour schemes – pale grey *toile de jouy*, walls papered with ladies playing tennis (which had no effect on my sporting abilities), a blue and white room, and eventually, at the age of seventeen, a pink and white room with all the bathroom fittings matching the curtain fabric. I remember thinking that this was the cleverest thing I'd ever seen.

If you are a person who loves the colour pink, as I was, then you must indulge yourself as a child or a young woman. The bedroom one has as a married woman can be pretty, but should not be too frilly – a room can be feminine without being too cloying for the other person. The walls in my

room are painted a sunny cream, as the background to the painted white trellis with arches at the top forming an arbour for the camellia trees which twine up it. Their white flowers, striped with crimson, contrast with the dark green leaves. I added convolvulus in the corners, and the odd butterfly and bird. The overall effect is neutral and relaxing, but when the sun shines into this room it is really beautiful.

The dressing room and bathroom that lead off our bedroom are designed to be efficient and easy to organise. Our walk-in cupboard/ dressing room is really a narrow passage between the bedroom and the bathroom, with my clothes on one side and my husband's on the other. In the bathroom, which is narrow and rather dark, bare bulbs around the mirror give the maximum light, and the room glows with lacquer-coated viridian green paint that resembles malachite. The prints along one wall have mirrored frames, which play up the reflections of the light.

The atmosphere of my bedroom is one of calm. I travel a great deal, and I adore coming home to the welcome sight of my well-made bed with its plumped-up pillows. I have an incurable weakness for bed linen: you can change your mood and the feel of the room with different sheets, or even just different pillowcases. Femininity can be expressed in beautiful bed linens, even in a room that is not overtly frilly and fussy. I don't believe in bedspreads, as they are only there to be removed and there is never anywhere to put them, so I usually make an eiderdown in a material that ties in with the rest of the room. I also have blanket covers, which also make the bed look prettier. I have always loved beautiful things of good quality, and this is undoubtedly reflected in my indulgences in linen.

When I first went to Paris and became aware of the exquisite linens and inspired designs of Porthault, they were beyond my wildest dreams. I discovered that one could buy just the baby pillows and pillowcases – so with plain sheets and lots and lots of tiny pillows I could surround myself with the sublime Porthault aura. I ended up selling the Porthault line in London – but by then I had come to prefer the mixture of plain sheets and printed cases. The only difference was that I had graduated to having the large square French pillows as well. My favourite combination is real linen sheets, which have the most marvellous feel, with pintucked and belaced pillowcases with a large frill on the edges.

My first shop was largely based on pillowcases, although it developed into presents, objects and anything to make people feel at home even in new surroundings. I am now longing to produce my own collection of bed linen, which will combine all the preferences that have evolved over my fifteen years of experimenting, and I hope it may happen next year.

During a recent visit to Milan, the taxi deposited me at a very unlikely looking address, and I arrived on the third floor to be faced with a large, uncommunicative Italian who showed me into a room full of hotel linen. Imagine my surprise and delight when the Signora started to show me samples, opening mahogany cupboards to reveal linens of every shape, size and description, each more delicious than the last. Even the drying-up cloths were right – the proper old-fashioned sort that don't leave those

Mother and daughter in Henrietta's bedroom, decorated with Nina Campbell's own fabrics and wallpaper. The chintzes have a green and blue floral design and a criss-cross pattern of twisted pink ribbon. The curtains sweep up to a coronet over the Empire bed; the window has a festoon blind.

awful bits on glass. People sometimes ask me how I can cope with my business, the travelling and my family, but it is these moments of discovery that compensate for the delayed planes, the early starts and the days when I cannot be with the children.

For my elder daughter, Henrietta, any colour will do as long as it's pink, preferably with hearts. Luckily, I went through the pink heart stage myself, and, failing to find a fabric on sale which fulfilled my fantasy, I had some printed – so Henrietta is well catered for in this love of hers. While we were away during the holidays I had Henrietta's bedroom re-decorated in a scheme from my new range of fabrics and wallpapers. This was partly to reassure myself that the collection worked, and partly as a surprise present for her. Of course it had to be in pink. I'm not sure which of us got the greatest pleasure, when I saw on her face the instant appreciation and disbelief at the transformation. I think that for a few moments she thought she was in the wrong house. Her room is now a

Bare bulbs around the mirror light the lacquered green bathroom that leads off the bedroom.

wonderful mixture of the remains of the little girl, with her appliquéd pictures, ornaments and endless bears and animals, and the beginnings of the young girl, with her dressing-table, hair ribbons and photographs – and the foundation of the young woman, with the French daybed and some lovely eighteenth-century prints.

If I had lived in the eighteenth century I would have held levées in my bedroom, as I think of it as the centre of family life. My desk, in the bay window, is covered with photographs of the children. I never give up out-of-date pictures, but I have kept on adding new ones, so there is not much room to work on the desk any more. The television is also in my room, so at weekends the whole family ends up in bed together, watching their favourite programmes. I shall have to stop having children, as it is becoming rather a squash! My telephones are on either side of the bed, so that both my husband and I can talk at the same time if necessary. One line has a number that only he knows, so that he can ring me late at night when he is away; it only rings in my room, and no-one else is woken up.

Whatever each day brings – a difficult client, a flood in the office, four of my staff all leaving at once, or Alice's second birthday party – my own bedroom is my refuge. For me, getting into bed and leaning against the soft pillows ought to be the prize at the end of a hard day. It is in this moment of calm before sleeping, when I have finished with books, magazines, or the notes I am writing to myself and others, that I feel in a state of total equilibrium.

Objects in inlaid wood on a marquetry table opposite the bed in the main bedroom.

SHEILA PICKLES

Sheila Pickles is the managing director of Penhaligon's, a small exclusive English perfume house, which she took over in 1975 to revive a dying business. Before that she lived in Italy, where she was private secretary to the film director Franco Zeffirelli for five years. She is married to David Rainer, a computer consultant, and they have two children. Their home is an eighteenth-century terraced house in Canonbury, London.

Three years ago we found our house and married, and for the first time in my life I had to consider someone else's taste and requirements in planning the interior. I did not like it at all. During the years I worked in Italy with Franco Zeffirelli I had acquired a taste for layer upon layer of fabric, and I had indulged my every whim in the decoration of my bedroom in the past: curtained beds, frills and flounces, cushions and shawls. Nothing was too much for me in my bachelor bliss, with only the comfort of my cats to consider. All that was to change. I had married a man who preferred greater simplicity, and I very quickly realised that the only way we could ever live happily side by side was by compromise. The bedroom is a very good example of it. We have probably ended up with a room neither of us would have achieved individually, but I think that it contains the best of us both, the result of my encouraging David and his restraining me.

The house is in a leafy north London cul-de-sac, and our bedroom looks out onto a mediaeval tower and a mulberry tree said to have been planted by Thomas Cromwell. It is the only place I have ever found in London with the feeling of a cathedral close, and as we lie in bed in the morning we see the sunshine through the leaves shining onto the old red brick.

There are three long windows, all with the original shutters. These are

Sheila Pickles in bed; nearby, a Victorian mahogany cradle. On the circular table in the foreground is an arrangement of silver family treasures.

Over the mantelpiece, a painting of Sheila Pickles' family home in Yorkshire.

following pages
Seen from the bed, a view of the tall windows flanked by two upright chairs and a pair of variegated Benjamina trees. The shuttered windows have frames and woodwork painted white and white Italian linen curtains.

in fact very practical, for we can close the lower half for privacy but leave the top half open to enjoy the morning. I had resigned myself to living without curtains as we could never agree on the fabric, but on a trip to Venice we suddenly spotted it in a draper's shop and the old Venetian draper made them for us overnight. We had bought just six lengths to hang on either side of the three windows, and once they were up we were disappointed, because the effect was skimpy. A few months later we saw 'Davidsbündlertanze' danced by the New York City Ballet, and realised how marvellous the long flimsy white curtains in that set looked covering the whole wall. Fortunately good friends were going to Venice the next month, and were persuaded to buy two more panels from the shop – for which we had neither a name nor an address. I drew the cherubs so that the fabric could be identified, and they returned with the curtains two weeks later saying that our directions ('It's on the way from the Accademia to the Rialto') had been faultless.

We chose a mid-blue carpet throughout the house (in the days before small muddy feet were a consideration) and selected soft subtle paint colours with the help of Jocasta Innes, who then transformed the walls with her magical techniques. She colour-washed the bedroom in pale terracotta, giving a warm peaceful feel to the room which was also very pretty. For me design and aesthetic appeal are more important than comfort and practicality, but the latter won the day when my brass bed was discarded in favour of my husband's large, low divan. I begged my Yorkshire aunts to give us their linen sheets, which I knew had long been put away in favour of something easier to launder. I only like white bed linen, and my mother edged all the linen pillowcases for my trousseau with tatting and old lace which had been made for the trousseau of her grandmother, Granny Maude.

I had the happiest of childhoods, and I love to be surrounded by those memories. If I wake in the night I am immediately comforted by the ticking of the old family grandfather clock, its friendly chimes telling us the hour, and above the mantelpiece is a watercolour of Carr House, where I grew up, and where the family had lived for generations. I commissioned the painting from a local artist some years ago and requested that he paint it on an overcast day to give the feeling of the thundery northern weather I remembered best. He was rather apologetic when it was finished, saying that it had turned out rather bigger than he expected – 'in fact sky's so big I 'ad t' paint it with pastry brush' – but he had certainly succeeded. The long room at the side was my nursery, which had a huge bell outside the window which Granny Maude used to ring to call the farm workers in to lunch.

I love to have my family round me. In this room I keep photographs of the different generations, and above the bed is my wedding bouquet, which my sister retrieved from the friend to whom I had carefully thrown it, and lovingly pressed the flowers and made them into a picture.

We consciously left the room quite sparsely furnished in order to maintain the spacious peaceful feeling, but the few pieces of furniture we have are mahogany and have been picked up on various antique hunts.

There is a chaise longue which was an old favourite of mine, but the cats had ruined the original charming faded chintz. We never have time to shop together in London, and once again it was when we were on holiday, this time in France, that we found the fabric in Bergerac just as the shop was shutting for the weekend. The glazed chintz has a pink and blue Florentine flame-stitch pattern which echoes the colour of the walls and carpet. We were nervous in case we had remembered the colours incorrectly, but decided to risk it. It was an instant decision, but happily the right one.

Next to the bedroom, and joined by an internal door, is what should be the spare room. We have greedily claimed it for ourselves, and it has become an extension of our bedroom. It is the room to which I escape if David is playing bridge or watching television, and where I can get on with my hobbies. It is important for me to be surrounded by my clutter, and the room houses old friends such as my 1912 sewing machine, a very old portable typewriter, gardening catalogues, half-finished tapestries, photograph albums, upholstery materials, toys and jigsaws. I love to spend whole evenings here on my own, and it is a luxury not to have to tidy away the half-finished project, but to shut the door on it and leave it for another occasion.

We never take work into the bedroom. After the babies were born I had a desk in the dressing room and worked at home, which I hope never to do again. I never felt able to get away from it; it was always sitting there on my desk waiting to be finished and I felt guilty if I did not keep returning to it. Perhaps because our bedroom is the room I use for relaxation, it seemed a violation of our life together to work there. During the day terrific demands are made on my time, and getting the balance right and keeping everyone happy is a continual problem. I feel constantly pulled between Penhaligon's shops, factory, outlets abroad, home and family. So our bedroom is the room to which I retreat to have some time to myself and recoup my energy.

I love to go to bed early, and if I am in on my own I sometimes take supper up to bed on a tray for a treat and use my bedtable. It is one of the old cane sort made by the blind. I wish I could bring myself to use it more often, but I cannot relax in bed unless all the jobs on my list have been crossed off and the family fed and settled. Once in the bedroom, however, I enjoy myself. I have a kettle and a large supply of green tea, I listen to Radio Three, chat on the telephone and read. There are large bookcases in the bedroom but in addition there are always piles of books on the table, the desk and our bedside tables; thrillers and books on bridge and fishing for David, biographies, gardening books and Virago authors for me. There is always a large pile of magazines by the bed which are scattered each morning when James arrives. We gave him for Christmas a life-size sheep on rockers which lives in our bedroom for those early morning visits, but he much prefers to play with the water spray which I use daily on the variegated Benjamina trees. Our happiest days together are spent gardening, and we bring as much of the garden as we can into the house, growing flowers which complement the colours of the rooms.

I am an early morning person and David is definitely a night owl, so we rarely talk in bed. He loves to spend Sunday morning in bed with the newspapers, but being a puritan I cannot enjoy them in bed in the morning, knowing all there is to do. I usually open them about midnight, with the result that they remain with us in the bedroom all week.

Sir Basil and Lady Spence used to live in this house, and they had a door knocked through into the house next door where he had his architectural practice. We were told that he used to go through in the mornings in his pyjamas to get the post, and run back again when he heard the key in the door. I have never been able to return to any of my homes once I have left, because the memories are too painful. But Lady Spence came to tea earlier this year and I showed her round the house and garden. She wrote to me afterwards that she felt no sadness at all, only happiness that her old home was loved and cared for.

Off-white linen Roman blinds at a small window in the bathroom. On the marble surface below the mirror are a group of silver-topped brushes and a collection of elegant bottles of scent from Penhaligon's.

LISA ST AUBIN DE TERÁN

Prize-winning novelist Lisa St Aubin de Terán lives in a Victorian Gothic folly built around an original fifteenth-century gatehouse in the Norfolk fens with her husband, poet and author George MacBeth, and their two children, Iseult and Alexander.

The bedroom is the arena of our dreams. The bed itself – described in one of R. L. Stevenson's poems as the 'little boat' – can easily become the magic galleon or the ocean-going liner in which we voyage at speed or at ease down the currents of the unconscious. We are born in bed, we sleep there, we die in bed. Each morning we step out of bunk or four-poster into a world made new, a real world, but one still linked inside the bedroom door to the mysterious, awe-inspiring world of our dreams.

Outside, the cooing pigeon circles, and within, the flames leap in the grate and the walls mirror the pictures in the coal and the iridescence in their spread wings. This happens at Wiggenhall St Mary the Virgin, anyway, where I pass my nights and my days waking to the sound of fluttering birds and dozing within the aura of flickering flames, the shadows dark as antlers in the Victorian ironwork.

Around the house there are goldcrests, nesting at the foot of an angleshaft, moving to and fro on the edge of vision like tropical fish. Beyond them, as I lean from under a cover of silk worked with Arabs and camels, I catch a glimpse of the pregnant peahen as she ruffles her feathers on the roof of our broken-down Scimitar. Jealous, her mate with a hundred eyes is shaking rain from his fan. He screams, and I rise, nudging ashes with a bare toe as I flit for the new loo in the fifteenth-century turret.

Romance – almost of a Mills and Boon kind – may seem to come easily in a bedroom lodged at the far end of a miniature Pre-Raphaelite castle, which is what my husband and I dreamed our way into an incautious year ago. Romance, though, is bought for a price, and one learns to match the reality of hods and stoking to the Clark Gable element of making love on a chaise longue under a flattering caress of shadows. I choose, each winter night, whether to stumble to my brass and golden cage by the light of a candle, or in the gentle glow of shaded bulbs, electric yet subtle. After all, there are times when I read a book, or even mark a proof, listening to the wind howling through the willow with a hot-water bottle between my knees, and it helps to have a hard clear shine on the page. There is a discipline in the steady gutter of a standard white candle as it wanes inexorably towards the socket – urging the eye and the hand forward over typescript or freckled sheet – but I lack the temperament to enjoy being pinned down by Time. I am very haphazard about where I write, and almost anywhere will do – sometimes on the chaise longue, sometimes lying in bed. But when work is in view, I prefer the inexhaustible glimmer of electricity.

The pleasures obtainable while sharing a bed I find even more delightful by candle and firelight. If I were not a novelist, or a farmer, I would like to stare into a bedroom fire professionally. Even incurable firewatchers like myself have to stand back from a furnace, but a bedroom grate is small enough to flicker and glow for hours.

So much for light and heat. So much for the world outside the window, the passing wings of birds. Two senses gone already, what price the other three? Well, I do, I confess, enjoy a drink in bed, whether a chaste and unsweetened mug of morning tea or a coruscating midnight snifter of Remy Martin. It helps to have someone to bring them in, too: my lanky eleven-year-old daughter Iseult in her pink shift with the Orange Pekoe, and – well, who shall we say? Paul Newman? – with the brandy. Sipping tea, I waken; savouring my brandy, I can get in the mood – for sleep, for dreams, for fantasy.

Above my head I look into a stained, shadowing raft of timbers, the dark hull of the boat I seem to be upside down in. The rain, like the waters of the Orinoco, laps on the slates only a few feet away. Sometimes, indeed, on a night of awful storms, it will force an intrepid drop or two through my protesting ceiling and into – exactly into, I always hope – a Minton jug on perpetual leak duty beside the skirting board.

I love fresh flowers in my bedroom – scented ones. When I first went out to Venezuela I put fresh lilies in my bedroom there, and I was told by the peasants that I had put the sign of death in the room. Since then, rather morbidly, I admit, I particularly like lilies of all sorts by my bed. The occasional spider is an unwelcome visitor to the strip of floor beyond my Aylsham sale carpet. A hornet was once excavated, in a pessimism of autumnal slowness, on a window sill. Three cats – a black, a delicious grey and a brindled mother – come in and out at their feline will. I do the same myself. One has to. But on the whole the animal life in this most private and slumberous cavern of an old house is courteously human. Kids, by appointment, that is, after knocking, and not before seven-thirty. I don't think my baby son, Alexander, remembers the time when his own

147

Victorian brass cot was strapped to my bed and he shared this room of ours. He delights now in transferring the heap of necklaces in my jewel box from sill to sill, and also finds the sheer height of the bed exciting. Meanwhile, Iseult has reached the stage where she barters my clothes from me.

My husband, George, a Japanophile complete with silk kimono and a collection of swords (but who, incongruously, hates rice) comes like the Greeks, bearing gifts. Fortunately he adores, as I do, the endless quirky splendours of nineteenth-century antiques, and he will devote hours to the folding of bombazine and the unbuttoning of elbow-length calf gloves. I have a passion for Edwardian dresses, which I buy and hoard almost compulsively. In my bedroom I indulge all my fantasies and it is the one room where I insist on being thoroughly spoilt. Under my bed are trunks of photographs, and in two of my glove drawers I keep two of my favourite unanswered letters – I never answer letters, as such, but I save them, as I save everything from bus tickets to grocery bills. George accepts the clutter, although disapprovingly, and he admits the need for a spill of silk and lace from old cases. He bought me once, for my birthday, a vanity case from the 1890s, which I keep under its rain cover beside my chest of drawers.

Rain. It seems to be a theme. Sun, though, is a frequent visitor to this eastward room, which boasts a second window to the full south, thus allowing a sleepy late riser to wake in full sunlight. Clocks and boxes tail away along the sills, and ivy – too much, too much, I always say, but I do nothing – coils relentlessly up the Norman glass of the window to my right.

The bed, you see, has been arranged in a staunch diagonal, like an arrow drawn back by the bow formed of the two walls with the south and east windows, and thus one lies with a view to either hand, a view of stars, or a scud of Norfolk cloud. Of course it means that, curtainless, one might be watched from outside, but then one is often watched elsewhere, and in the wilds of the fens there are few Peeping Toms – or Prying Marys – with anything more shockable than a Springer spaniel or a split shotgun.

Indeed, the house – at any rate, on a grim day – has so much of the Hammer movie about its main façades that the unfamiliar local is inclined to give it rather a wide berth. Ghosts in the garden are fairly rare. (I've never seen one.) But the nanny claims to have noticed a maid with a cap and a coal scuttle emerge from her wardrobe and poke with resolution at an unmade fire. In my bedroom I lie alone at times and shiver. Sometimes it is because I need an extra blanket or the black fur rug, but sometimes it is because of noises in the dark.

There is no legend as such about the room, although it has a touch of direct history. In 1943 a returning German bomber dropped his remaining bomb-load into our grounds, and the resulting explosion tore down all the ceiling plaster, blew out the windows and made the north corner subside. Then the door was closed, and the debris left untouched for nearly forty years. This legacy of the war was what confronted us when we bought the place. My bedroom was definitely the most ruined

Lisa St Aubin de Terán on the chaise longue in her bedroom, wearing a Twenties' dress of paillettes and sequins designed by Worth, which she found in an antique shop in Yarmouth.

The bed is reflected in a mirror over the fireplace. The angles formed by the mullioned windows and the position of the bed make an interesting shape — like a bird with outspread wings. The dramatic bedhead is a tapestry screen draped with curtains in old dark red velvet.

room in all the ramshackle ruins of the house. It was the mixture of light, idiosyncrasy of shape and elegance under the decay that first attracted me to the room, and, I suppose, the isolation. No-one had groped their way through the cobwebs or disturbed the rubble, let alone slept there, since the time of the bomb.

So I brought the room from nothing, from a wreck, a chaos and a memory to what it is now. I rodded out the skeletons of dead birds from the chimney, and sackfuls of blackened twigs. I cannot know whether the two swaddled children, the last of the fifteenth-century Kervilles, whose alabaster effigies stand in the local church, were ever in my room, but I like to think so. Just as I don't know if in the eighteenth century Browne, the Italian Consul, went mad between the shafts of my two Gothic windows, or if Gustavus Helsham, the Pre-Raphaelite nut-case who built most of the present house around the fifteenth-century gatehouse, felt about my bedroom as I do, but again, I like to think he did. An old bedroom will always have a history, though, and one with its share of tragedies as well as births and bliss.

When I am depressed, I lie on my bed and listen to music – Grieg, Tchaikovsky, Elvis Presley – or, when I'm really in the pits – Marlene Dietrich. I will, however, also lie on my bed with a nineteenth-century novel and a cocktail when I am feeling particularly elated. On other days I pull out from under the bed my cases of family photographs and look at the old pictures, four generations of similar bones fading together.

I also get my best ideas in bed. Lying awake in the small hours I plot out my future books, holidays, plans, cruising to every corner of the globe. Usually I just drift on the journeys of my imagination, to seething waves as well as pleasant islands, the swine of Circe as well as the apples of the Hesperides. I accept them all. In the eight hours that I spend on average in here, I enjoy through my imagination the visitations of cultures deeper for me than any culled from library shelves. I sip the nectar of the Gods. I sleep and live. So bring me my Remy Martin, Mr Newman. Hand me my mug of tea, Iseult. And thank you, bedroom; thank you, bed.

A rich mixture of colours, appropriately Pre-Raphaelite, in a corner of the bedroom. A Victorian blue silk jacket hangs over the chair next to the chest of drawers, and above it an oil painting of the Pembrokeshire cliffs at Stackpole.